ning Exch

151 25

Social Work Process and Practice

D0476961

NUV 2010

Also by Janice West:

Social Work and the Law in Scotland (co-edited) *

*Also published by Palgrave Macmillan

Social Work Process and Practice: Approaches, Knowledge and Skills

David Watson and Janice West

Consultant editor: Jo Campling

First published in 2006 by
PALGRAVE MACMILLAN
Houndmills, Basingstoke, Hampshire RG21 6XS and
175 Fifth Avenue, New York, N.Y. 10010
Companies and representatives throughout the world.

PALGRAVE MACMILLAN is the global academic imprint of the Palgrave
Macmillan division of St. Martin's Press, LLC and of Palgrave Macmillan Ltd.
Macmillan® is a registered trademark in the United States, United Kingdom
and other countries. Palgrave is a registered trademark in the European
Union and other countries.

ISBN-13: 978–1–4039–0585–7
ISBN-10: 1–4039–0585–1

This book is printed on paper suitable for recycling and made from fully
managed and sustained forest sources.

A catalogue record for this book is available from the British Library.

A catalog record for this book is available from the Library of Congress.

10 9 8 7 6 5 4 3 2 1
15 14 13 12 11 10 09 08 07 06

Printed in China

Contents

List of Figures and Tables

Figures

Tables

Preface

This textbook emerges from our joint involvement in the learning and teaching of social work students and our increasing awareness of the complexity and diversity of social work practice confronting them in the twenty-first century. Nothing seems to remain unchanged for any significant period of time; new legislation, changing social attitudes, organisational restructuring all add to the feelings of uncertainty and challenge as new workers enter this their profession of choice. Adaptability and flexibility are core skills that need to be developed in order that they become effective practitioners and colleagues. How students negotiate their way through this constantly changing professional landscape is a significant challenge. In a world of increasing proceduralisation, integrated service delivery and interprofessional working, social workers are seeking to retain their unique professional identity. For many, the development of a professional identity takes place over time and may involve an element of trial and error. What this book aims to provide is a framework within which those evolutionary processes can take place in a planned and structured manner. It is our central thesis that while workers need to develop an understanding of the core knowledge, skills and values that underpin this professional activity, they also need to have an appreciation of the agency and policy context within which they work. How these issues are understood and internalised by individual workers will inform their approach to practice. In our view, every worker has a specific approach to how he or she practises. For some, this may be more explicit and clearly understood than for others. Implicit or explicit, all workers have an approach to their practice.

It is the intention of this book to explore how our approach impacts on our abilities as social workers and the service we provide. To this end, Chapter 1 sets the overall context for modern practice, exploring the importance of process and outcome on service delivery. Chapter 2 explores what we mean by approach and the main responses prevalent in social work at this point in time. It also considers the factors that influence the worker's approach and asks readers to consider whether their own desired approach is consistent with their present practice. The theme of the worker's approach carries into the remaining chapters of the book, which examine the social work process, through from assessment to implementation, evaluation and termination. In this context Chapter 3 considers the process of assessment as it relates to intervention and practice, including care management. In particular, it examines how risk assessment and partnership have impacted on the assessment process and what skills the worker requires to undertake an assessment that empowers the service user.

Chapter 4 explores the relationship between assessment and method selection. It is the contention of this chapter that workers need to utilise a range of methods, thereby ensuring that practice fits the users' needs rather than merely the worker's knowledge, skills and values. The impact of organisational culture on the purpose and importance of methods is considered. The use of contracts is discussed in relation to the potential to liberate or regulate service user empowerment. Chapters 5 and 6 examine the main methods used by social work practitioners, including the task-centred, behavioural, crisis intervention and psychosocial methods. The underpinning theory, assessment process, structure of intervention and termination and evaluation of each method is considered. The applicability of each method to the approaches outlined in Chapter 2 is evaluated. Chapter 7 considers the factors involved in selecting a method of intervention, including the worker's approach, the service user's needs and abilities and agency context. The issue of involving and empowering service users who have had negative (or involuntary) experience of social work services is explored. This chapter concludes by looking at the often undervalued skill of decision-making and what influence this has on the worker's practice.

Chapter 8 considers the importance of reflection in developing the process of good practice. It examines the stages and models of reflection that students and practitioners can expect to encounter in their practice. It also considers the role of both practice learning and the workplace supervisory relationship in the development of professional decision-making. In this context the skills of administration and organising others are explored, particularly as they relate to the student/worker's personal empowerment and professionalism. Chapter 9 explores the issue of evaluation of service from two contrasting perspectives: effectiveness of intervention and purposeful termination of involvement. In terms of effectiveness, the use of single case evaluation as part of an empowering and partnership approach to enable service users to reflect and be part of this process is discussed. The process of termination is also examined in terms of the methods employed, the worker's approach and the agency context. The last chapter in this book revisits the issue of the worker's approach and its potential application within different agency and service-user situations. In particular, it emphasises the necessity for students and workers to continue to develop their approach in the post-qualifying context at both a formal and an informal level if they are to remain empowering and effective practitioners.

Throughout the text, case studies have been used as a device to assist the reader to locate the concepts being discussed within a practice context. There are four case studies utilised and we hope that Susan, John, Brian and Sandeep will become increasingly familiar to you as the text progresses. This will, we hope, demonstrate the inter-connectedness of the subject matter in the chapters and the importance of process within social work. As each new case study is introduced, a synopsis of the situation is provided, which is then enhanced and developed as new issues or concepts are explored. Each has been selected to represent a set of issues and is an amalgam of many situations encountered over the years. By focusing upon the same people throughout, we hope to illustrate how social work intervention needs to be flexible and responsive if it is indeed to become effective and ethical.

The emphasis throughout the text is on the process of social work intervention. It does not seek to be prescriptive but rather is a contribution to the ongoing development of understanding of the interaction between worker and service user in social work contexts.

Acknowledgements

This book emerges from a consultation with Jo Campling in 2002 and would not have reached this final stage without her advice, encouragement and support.

As collaborative teachers, we owe much to the feedback of our students who over the years have helped us to refine the ideas we seek to present within this text. Particular thanks are due to those colleagues and students who took the time to read various drafts of chapters as they evolved – Moira McGeoch, Elaine Rae and Julie McKenzie. Their thoughtful and insightful comments helped steer us on a better path. Any remaining errors are, however, our responsibility.

Thanks are also due to Gordon Morlan for his technical skills in preparing the manuscript and to Catherine Gray and her team at Palgrave Macmillan for their advice and support. Finally, any work of this nature takes its toll on one's domestic life. This book could not have been written without the unflagging support, goodwill and understanding of our respective children – Lindsay and Graeme West, Derek and Poppy Watson.

1

New Professionalism: The Challenge for Social Work Practice

Practice that can be evidenced as ethical and effective is a central feature of modern social work. It is embraced by both the professional and policy agendas and is emblematic of social work in the twenty-first century. Like most aspirations, it is open to interpretation and refinement by workers and by the agencies in which they are employed. In this context, ethical and effective practice is frequently confused with the emerging 'what works' agenda (McGuire and Priestley 1995) that reflects the need to justify outcomes, not only for the service user but often in terms of value for money. Good practice, from a professional perspective, is about more than effectiveness; it is also concerned with *how* outcomes are achieved – the ethical. What this means is that practice that is understood to be ethical and effective is likely to be moderated through both the individual worker's approach and the agency context. This raises issues over 'what works' for whom, why and in what way. For example, for front-line workers, 'what works' may mean meeting agency standards and government targets rather than responding to individual service users' needs. Alternatively it may help workers to set more realistic and achievable goals, enabling those using the service to feel valued and empowered to make choices. Therefore, whilst the criteria for measuring 'what works' may be contested, what underpins good practice with service users is less open to challenge. Workers need to be open and honest about their role and what can and cannot be achieved, working in partnership with both other agencies and service users to achieve that end. At the heart of this way of working is listening to what those using the service have to say, taking account of both their thoughts and their feelings, in relation not only to what is to be achieved, but also the manner in which it is to be done. In effect, ethical and effective practice includes consideration of how the

1

service is delivered as well as the achievement of outcomes. This is a point of view shared by service users themselves who, according to NISW (1996), value workers who respect them as people not problems and are open and honest about what they can do in practice.

When we start to consider good practice it becomes apparent that it is both ethical, in that the manner and means of creating change is important, and effective, in that it should achieve agreed outcomes between the service user and worker. In this context,

ethical practice requires workers to incorporate:

- a strong, empowering value base which incorporates an awareness of the worker's approach to practice and how this impacts on service delivery;

- anti-discriminatory and anti-oppressive principles;

- accountability – both personal and professional.

Effective practice involves:

- a theoretical understanding of both the workers' and the service users' actions within a particular socioeconomic context;

- an understanding of the relevant current research evidence;

- a clear process of evaluation which incorporates the service user perspective.

Ethical Practice

Social work values, as Dominelli (2002a, p. 16) suggests, are 'socially constructed and historically specific'. This means that interpretations of what constitutes an appropriate value base for social work practice changes and evolves to meet the changing nature of the service environment. That process of change has been rapid in recent years (Mitchell 2000) but the emphasis on values and the associated ethical codes remains strong. Given that much of social work intervention takes place with individuals and groups within society who are disadvantaged and potentially vulnerable, it is, in our view, important for workers to be aware of their own values and how these may impact on the service user. The values held by workers will influence their approach to practice, as some approaches may be inconsistent with particular value stances. It is not our intention to explore values in detail, as these are more than adequately covered in other texts (Banks 2001, 2004; Shardlow 2002). Social work values must, if they are to be meaningful in terms of partnerships with service users, take account of the impact of power within such relationships and we therefore wish to focus on empowerment as a fundamental social work value.

Empowerment in our experience is rarely a straightforward or simple activity for social workers. How it is defined and applied can have clear consequences for both workers and service users. In practice it has the potential to be used either as a subtle means of controlling behaviours or, more positively, can lead to a transformation of the use of power in order that service users have a greater say over the decisions affecting their lives (Beresford and Wilson 2000). Our concern is that, in the world of practice, all too often workers and their organisations individualise the concept, thereby locating the sources of disempowerment in the service user and empowerment in the worker. This is a perspective on empowerment that can lead social workers and service users to believe that the root cause of the problem is centred on them rather than on how society and its institutions are organised and structured. Service users in this model of empowerment, are often viewed as problematic and expected to use their limited power to fit into more 'socially acceptable' ways of responding and behaving.

The alternative to the individual approach has been termed 'democratic empowerment'. This democratic approach places structural oppression and disadvantage, and consequently collective ways of challenging existing power through anti-oppressive practice, at the centre of its analysis (Pugh and Thompson 1999). In this approach, empowerment centres not only on changing services but also on how service users are perceived and provided for by the wider society. Integral to this approach are the service users themselves, deciding upon their own services. It therefore avoids definitions of empowerment that can become expressions of professional and organisational power over users (Adams 1996). Payne (1997, p. 266) provides a good working definition for this approach when he says that empowerment is about helping, 'clients gain power of decisions and action over their own lives by reducing the effects of social or professional blocks to exercise the existing power, by increasing the capacity and self confidence to use power and by transferring power from environment to clients'. This definition challenges the notion that empowerment is something that workers do to service users and possibly that managers do to workers 'thus allowing the powerful to maintain control of the process' (Barry 1998, p. 2). Empowerment in this definition and application is not a gift to be bestowed on service users and therefore it is not in the power of social workers or their organisation to confer (Anderson 1996). Consequently, empowerment involves more than the powerful worker relinquishing power, it is also about locating service users within their structural context and the oppression and inequality that can ensue. Within this approach, empowerment is perceived as a process and a goal rather than an event, a process that Dalrymple and Burke (1995) argue is underpinned by collaboration between the service user and the worker working in partnership. The worker therefore needs to acknowledge and utilise the capabilities and expertise of service users individually and collectively to effect change (DuBois et al. 1992). This democratic approach to empowerment provides an integrity and value base that enables social work to redefine itself as an activity in the modern state. It is also about workers moving beyond uncritical, reactive practice to sharing their knowledge and skills with those with whom they are working. Implicit in this approach is acknowledging that all service users, no matter how disadvantaged or oppressed, have a contribution to make to the resolution of their situation. What is crucial to this process of empowerment is that workers start to reflect upon their knowledge base, skills and values in order that they can look to improve their own practice. We should ensure that we are not fitting service users to our value base but conversely understanding that we as workers have the skills, knowledge and abilities to provide a service that fits the service users' needs. This has meant a redefining of professional social work and the notion of formal expertise and the control of power to incorporate more liberating and effective ways of practice that put the service user at the heart of the decision-making process (Lymbery 2004). Whilst emphasising the importance of democratic empowerment to good practice, we are not arguing that there is only one way to undertake the professional activity of social work. There are undoubtedly a number of approaches to practice within the modern social work environment, as we shall explore in the next chapter.

Social work is practised within a range of settings and is increasingly undertaken as part of integrated service delivery systems. This diversity occurs partly because utilisation of knowledge and skills is a contested activity in social work that enables different interpretations and values stances to be adopted. It is also due to the complex situations faced by those using the service confronting multiple oppressions on a daily basis. Even in the most straightforward of interactions with service users, workers have to be able to understand what the service users' experience means for them and how this perception is influenced and shaped by the nature of the wider community and society. Workers therefore need knowledge of how people function, their support networks and how society can influence and impact on everyday lives. This will be influenced for both worker and service user alike by 'differences of class, race, gender, age, disability, sexual orientation, religion, culture, health, geography, expectations and outlook on life' (Trevithick 2000, p. 2). These issues rarely, if ever, have straightforward explanations and understandings that can be agreed upon or universally applied. It is into this contested territory that good practice has to be understood and applied. Central to this is the acknowledgement that society is characterised by social injustice and that the role of the worker is to try to eradicate this, 'at least those forms of it which are reproduced in and through social work practice' (Dominelli 1998, p. 5). This is predicated on enabling service users, as far as possible, to have a say over the decisions that affect their lives and the way they should live. It is also a practice that requires a skilled response on the part of the worker to what are rarely simple or straightforward situations.

Social work practice does not take place in a vacuum in which workers are the sole arbiters of what is provided. While the professional integrity of individual workers is important, it is also influenced by both the agency and the society in which it is located. Arguably, modern social work is at a difficult junction between two competing ways of working that are often contradictory and conflicting in relation to each other. These are the growing clarity of 'new' professional practice, with its aim of empowering those using the service to effect change, and the influence of managerialism on organisation and service delivery. Workers do not practise independently but represent and act for the organisations in which they are employed. This has implications for the level of discretion and autonomy available in their daily practice (Hugman 1991; White 1999). Social work organisations are increasingly adopting an organisational ethos that reflects the ideas and values of managerialism with its top-down control of the decision-making and change processes (Clarke and Newman 1997). Whilst we are not in principle against the changes associated with managerialism, we are sceptical about its claim to create more efficient and effective services and are concerned about its effect on the development of an empowering practice. For example, the inclusion of service users and providers in the decision-making process closely fits the growing professional paradigm of empowerment and the wider value base of social work. Equally, the emphasis on the importance of changing ethos and culture to improve service fits closely with the notion of anti-oppressive practice and its analysis of societal and community influences (Dickens 1995; Adams 1998). In addition, the move towards clarity of expectation and desire to meet the customers' or service users' needs fits with the growing practice of partnership, contracts and access to information presently impacting on social work (Adams 1996, 1998). However, it is when applying these concepts in the top-down culture created by managerialism that the closeness of fit with empowering professional practice becomes more difficult to sustain and support.

This top-down, regulatory culture often means that the professional autonomy and decision-making of workers are colonised by strategic managers within the organisation of the local state (Clarke and Newman 1997).

The effect of this colonisation, as Parton and O'Byrne (2000, p. 44) point out, is 'ever more sophisticated systems of accountability and thereby attempts to rationalise increasing areas of social work activity via the activity of increasingly complex procedures and systems of audit – whereby it is assumed that the world can be subject to prediction and calculation'. Consequently, the decision-making role of the worker has increasingly been taken over by managers who decide the best ways of implementing policies within a particular context. According to Flynn (1997, p. 40), the right to manage in this context is 'the right to tell people what to do and expect them to do it'. It is not based on democratic empowerment but hierarchical structures that limit the abilities of workers to respond to situations and thus increase the control of management. The impact of these changes has arguably been systematically to undermine the autonomy of the individual social worker. This is discussed by Dominelli and Hoogvelt (1996), who argue that the social work process is increasingly being broken down into small and routinised tasks which are then seen as outwith the professional remit and consequently can be carried out by workers with limited training and skills. This process is particularly apparent in relation to intake or duty systems, which are increasingly being redefined as 'receiving services', leading to new referrals being assessed in the first instance by unqualified workers (Watson 2002). In effect, managerialism can lead to a diminution of professional social work, as it fits a much more procedural and performance measurement perspective that is concerned with scrutiny, accountability and outcomes rather than emancipating those receiving the service. Our view is that, despite the inherent difficulties, social work and social workers must begin to assert the empowering practice agenda. This 'new professionalism' presents a considerable challenge to social work practice in the twenty-first century. Social work intervention is now taking place within an organisational culture that does not necessarily lend itself to democratic forms of empowerment and may even at times challenge the core values of social work as a professional discipline. In this respect we are not suggesting the notion of professionalism of social workers as aloof experts, but instead see social work as a professional activity based on working alongside service users and enabling them to take more control of their lives. An intention of this book is to explore how empowering practice can be achieved and to begin to address the challenges posed not just by managerialism but also by service users and their situations.

What this anti-oppressive ethos does bring to the fore for workers is the need to reflect upon and review their practice on an ongoing basis. Whilst this poses many challenges, it should hopefully guard against uncritically accepting 'the way it is done' which has gained credence over recent years, usually based on folklore and local custom. Our concern is that in this commonsense approach, ethical and effective practice occurs at best by chance rather than by design as workers constantly react to situations rather than reflect upon and plan their interactions with service users and other agencies. It also diminishes the role of formal learning (Trevithick 2000) and means that practice is rarely reviewed for its effectiveness or whether it enables service users to have a greater say over their lives. Whilst thinking on one's feet, a key component of this commonsense approach, is undoubtedly an important social work skill, it is not the main determinant of professional practice. Ethical and effective practice requires workers to utilise a range of skills and to incorporate knowledge obtained from both practice and theoretical learning. It requires them constantly to review their values and reflect on how these are impacting on work at all levels. In essence, ethical and effective social work practice becomes a process of thought and reflection as well as action that considers how to provide a high-quality service.

These difficulties and uncertainties are typified by Susan's situation. We shall return throughout the text to this case study to help illustrate particular aspects of practice. She, like the other case studies used in this book, represents an amalgam of the many families we have worked with over the years.

Susan's Story

Susan, a 23-year-old woman with two children, was referred to social work services by the family health visitor following a suicide attempt. During the initial visit by the social worker it came to light that Susan was a lone parent who had started to suffer postnatal depression following the birth of her second child six months earlier. She and the children lived in a small, privately rented flat which was sparsely decorated. In essence, Susan lived in only one room with her children as she was afraid to allow them into the other areas of the house because of her concerns that they might hurt themselves. Susan had accumulated considerable debts over the previous three years and owed money to all the utility companies and to a series of credit card companies. She had little family support in the area and could see no point to her life as she had been virtually confined to the family home for the previous six months. She was unable to get the children into nursery school and was physically run down as a result of having little or no respite. She also had a number of other physical and emotional health problems that were being treated at the local health centre.

Susan's world reflects the complex lives of people using social services, few of whom are referred with single, easily resolved problems. Instead, as with Susan, their problems are complex and interrelated in a way that makes their resolution difficult. For example, Susan's concerns regarding childcare were also tied in with her financial situation. Her debts and dependency on state benefit meant she could not afford safety equipment for her home. The consequence of this was her need constantly to attend to the care of her children. She felt that, like her own parents, she was providing a poor role model, as she was constantly chastising her children rather than spending fun time with them. This brief outline of Susan's situation raises questions that social workers have to deal with on a daily basis, particularly, in this situation, obtaining a balanced understanding of Susan's past and present and the factors that oppressed her in her social context. The worker involved in this case would also have to bridge an understanding between Susan and wider society and then find ways of working that did not leave her discriminated against because of the situation in which she found herself. From a feminist perspective, for example, Susan's situation as a lone female carer had more to do with structural oppression than with any individual issues she might have (Abbott and Wallace 1997). The starting point from this perspective would therefore be shaped by the need to challenge the patriarchal nature of the oppression impacting on Susan's life. However, given Susan's multiple concerns, other forms of analysis would be possible, which means that the nature of the work and its starting point would be difficult to determine. As a consequence, this often means that intervention, and the level of intervention required, need to be negotiated around the service users' perception of their situation if they are to feel confident and empowered.

Work between Susan and her social worker would not take place in a vacuum and would consequently also be influenced by agency policy, government guidance and statute. Any social worker involved in this situation would have to consider the wellbeing and welfare of the children, a complex task given that the information provided by the referrer would suggest that they were potentially at risk but also loved and cared for by their mother. In this context, Susan herself would have to be assessed and supported in terms of her ability to fulfil her roles and responsibilities in relation to her children. Social work support is no longer just about care, but also about control and the complex interplay of these two factors (Parton 1985). Working with Susan would, therefore, require the social worker to consider the issue of support and empowerment to help her develop as a person and create a better life for both herself and the children. However, it would also entail the need for vigilance in relation to the care and protection provided to the children, raising questions about the extent to which Susan could operate autonomously in terms of her actions and choices. The social worker might, therefore, consider that Susan's situation was less than voluntary (Trotter 1999). It is for these reasons that social work is such a complex activity, as it deals with the area of human experience of those suffering from multiple problems, many of which are arguably outwith the individual's own control. It is when we start to consider Susan's situation that it becomes apparent how difficult an activity social work is to define, operating in the contested, non-consensual world of how we perceive and organise our society.

Developing a Framework for Effective and Ethical Practice

Despite our belief that best practice is about making the links between individuals and the wider societal oppression they face, this book will adopt the individual worker as the focus of such practice. In adopting this stance we are not suggesting that workers should reject the macro, structural perspectives or political activities as a focus of social work practice. For example, from a worker's perspective, clearly the more controlling forms of managerialism require to be challenged directly, particularly when they detract from quality services and the ability of workers to develop empowering practice (Lymbery and Butler 2004). We are, however, arguing that micro work also has the potential to be anti-oppressive and empowering for those receiving the service. As Coulshed (1991, p. 3) points out, 'Human beings remain at the centre of our concern, the raison d'être of our enterprises; thus face-to-face work is a prominent part of social work practice.' How individual workers go about their task and the knowledge, skills and values they hold will impact on all aspects of their work, from the first contact with the service user to assessment, work over time, termination and evaluation. It is our view that in an occupation such as social work the *process* (what we do) is as important as the *outcome* (what is achieved). To ignore this is to fail to recognise the fundamental importance of the worker critically to influence people's lives.

The first step in this process of developing ethical and effective practice for the individual worker is examining his/her own personal development and how to go about acquiring the skills, knowledge and values to be the type of worker he/she wants to become. This is not a neutral process, but one that should reflect the worker's knowledge, understanding, awareness and motivation. In this respect, ethical and effective practice depends on what we think social work is about and how we go about trying to achieve that goal. Therefore, whilst not claiming to have definitive answers, we believe that it should include the following:

- acknowledging service users as individuals who are affected by structural forces that impact on their lives;

- acknowledging service users as experts in their own lives and building upon their strengths;

- being honest and open with realistic and achievable goals agreed by all;

- developing a skilled and knowledgeable practice that is open about the value stance of the worker;

- learning from others' experiences and observations – be it from research studies or descriptions of good individual practice;

- critically and constructively reviewing our own practice in order to generate more relevant and up-to-date practice research;

- evaluating from the perspective not just of the worker or agency but also of the service user.

Ethical and effective practice is about acquiring the necessary knowledge and values and developing the professional skill to implement these with a diverse range of service users. In other words it is about our approach to social work practice.

Summary of Chapter

1. Good practice is both effective and ethical, emphasising both process and outcome for the service user. It places the service user at the heart of the process of intervention.

2. How the worker interprets and applies core values such as empowerment is crucial to process of practice. Empowerment can be defined to either individualise the service user's situation or alternatively to include wider societal structures. Good practice would entail moving beyond individualising the service user and locating the problem with him/her to seeing the individual within a community/societal context.

3. Social work is influenced by the agency context, which creates challenges and limitations for workers. Arguably social work is at a crossroads between two competing paradigms – managerial and anti-oppressive. In this respect the managerial agenda has the potential to create an ethos that emphasises effectiveness and outcome at the expense of process and ethics. Its top-down nature can also be restrictive of democratic definitions of empowerment, as formal decision-making power is located in the higher echelons of the organisation. Workers need to assert the professional agenda in the context of their everyday practice to act as a counterbalance to the growing influence of managerialism.

4. Social work practice is rarely a straightforward activity, but instead is characterised by complexity related to a range of oppressions impacting on both the service user's and the worker's situation. Unthinking, reactive practice is not enough to meet service users' needs or provide a good service. Instead, good practice is a skilled activity where workers constantly reflect on their knowledge, skills and values to make sense of the complex situations that service users face.

2

Approaches to Practice

Social work as a professional activity is in danger of being subsumed into the more general arena of bureaucratic 'competence' as managerial systems seek to exert increasing control over the workforce (Jones 2001; Lymbery and Butler 2004). It falls therefore to those engaged in the task continually to assert its unique contribution as a care profession (Beresford 2001). The social work role and task is not simply about action and good intentions, laudable and important as these are for many people who need and require support in their lives. It is also about thinking, planning and empowering those using the service and it therefore needs workers to develop a conscious awareness of their own approach to practice. This should enable workers to be aware of how their own knowledge, skills and values impinge and impact on the service user's situation. By maintaining this level of artistry (Ruch 2000), workers are less likely solely to become caught up in the procedural imperatives of the managerial agenda. It is our view that the development of each worker's approach to practice requires to be undertaken in a reflective and deliberate manner, as this will underpin every other aspect of professional activity and process.

So what do we mean by an approach to practice? Essentially, it is about the workers' orientation to the task and how they use their knowledge, skills and values in practice. This will draw upon a number of different elements. Whilst this is by no means an exhaustive list, these include:

● an understanding of society and how it works;

● an understanding of wider political issues and agency agendas;

● an understanding of personal and professional values.

An understanding of society and how it works. As we shall discuss when we examine specific approaches in more detail, workers develop awareness during their professional training of a range of ways of understanding the individual within the context of the wider society. This enables them to build their own theoretical understanding of the interrelationship between the individual and society that will be influential in deciding about the causation of a particular area of difficulty in the individual's circumstances. An oversimplification would be to suggest that an understanding of society enables the worker to make a judgement about where responsibility for specific situations should rest. Howe (1987) suggests that there are two key questions that social workers need to answer in the context of the individual and society. The first is related to how you see people. Are they subjects who have free will and choice, or are they 'objects' who are controlled, responsive to the environment in which they reside. In essence, what is the psychological position that you hold? The second question is related to the nature of society, or how you consider sociological issues. Do you live in a society that supports and has rules and regulations, where people tend to pull together and are cared for, or do you live in a society where people are in conflict, where there is a constant striving for power and position. Is society regulated for all to benefit or does it reflect the needs and issues of the powerful? What is the sociological theory of society you hold? Making sense of these questions involves adopting a paradigm for practice – an approach to social work. All workers use theories, be it in the context of social work or of life in general. Therefore, it is better to be explicit about one's theory base and one's assumptions about people and society, so that these are open to scrutiny rather than hidden away and unaccountable. How you answer these questions and their interrelationship will shape how you see the world and, equally importantly, how you view the role and task of social work in working with those using the service (Howe 1987).

An understanding of wider political and agency issues can manifest itself in a number of ways when developing an approach to practice. Some workers will come to the social work task with a very clearly defined political perspective which shapes their understanding of the issues and situations they encounter. Others may be less overtly political but will still be influenced by the wider political climate. Given that much of the activity of social work practice is defined by statute (Braye and Preston-Shoot 1998), even the most apolitical of workers need to work with the consequences of political decisions. Each worker needs to make a personal judgement about how to respond to these political pressures, some of which are more subtle than others. Workers providing a service within the youth justice area, for example, may find themselves constrained by a political perspective that places the responsibility for all aspects of antisocial conduct with the individual offender. Such a perspective is likely to resource only those aspects of the social work response which relate directly to reducing reoffending, while the individual worker's perspective may be much more holistic (Waterhouse et al. 2004). In an environment where there is heavy emphasis and support for one particular perspective, workers will find it difficult to sustain an alternative world-view. This can lead to the development of a rather prescriptive response by workers who may cease to individualise complex situations owing to the narrow range of resource options available. In this respect the culture and organisation of the agency where the social work task is undertaken will also have an influence on the approach of the worker. Some agencies, particularly those in the voluntary sector which have a very specific remit, are able to articulate a very clear set of norms and expectations. Any worker employed by such an agency is likely to share these cultural expectations to some extent and these will set the parameters of acceptable approaches to practice. The difficulty for many workers is that the norms and expectations of social work organisations are not always clearly articulated to workers and the process of being absorbed into the culture of the organisation remains more subtle. What is important in this context is that workers operate in an environment that impacts on their ability both to define and to deliver a service. This is not to suggest that individual workers are not able to influence the service; clearly they are in practice. What is important is that they reflect on their political stance and its implications for themselves, the agency and the service user. Failure to do this may mean that workers unquestionably adopt an approach that reflects the needs of the agency, which may not necessarily be those of the service user. Alternatively it can mean that workers are unable to deliver the service that they have agreed with the service user, as it is not within their power to provide it. In working out this aspect of your approach, you are fundamentally asking questions about the kind of agency you want to work for, not just in terms of what it should provide but, more importantly, in terms of what it does provide.

An understanding of personal and professional values also plays a significant role in the development of an approach to practice. Every social worker needs to develop the ability to scrutinise his/her value base on an ongoing basis. The ability constantly to examine one's own values and their potential impact on service delivery is one of the crucial hallmarks of professional social work practice (Banks 2001). This is overlaid by standards and codes of practice that define expectations in terms of professional values (HMSO 2000; GSCC 2002). While these are set within particular parameters, they are not generally prescriptive, allowing for some degree of individual interpretation.

The currency of the knowledge base and how workers are able to use this constructively will also influence the approach to practice. The more expansive the range of knowledge from which workers can draw, the greater the choices in terms of their ability to apply their approach. Workers who actively maintain their current knowledge base and who retain an active interest in theory and research are, in our view, much less likely to adopt an uncritical, ill-defined approach to practice. Strategies for maintaining a culture of learning within practice will be explored more fully later in this text, but it is important at this point to emphasise the crucial role of critical reflection in the pursuance of a truly professional approach to practice (Schön 1987; Fook 2002). The approach to practice adopted by workers will influence the assessment process and the nature of any subsequent intervention. This means that each individual worker will respond uniquely to what may appear to be very similar sets of circumstances. It is part of the challenge of good social work practice to be able to articulate clearly the reasons for the many choices being made throughout the social work relationship. Good practice values the uniqueness of the individual and eschews the development of formulaic responses to situations. It would be our view that the approach to practice being adopted needs to be communicated clearly to service users if the relationship is to be truly participative and inclusive. Social work writers (Howe 1987; Payne 1997; Dominelli 1998) suggest that there are a number of ways in which approaches to practice can be categorised. We have chosen to identify three approaches which we consider to be prevalent across a range of social work agencies:

● the procedural approach;

● the individual pathology approach;

● the progressive approach.

As with any taxonomy, these are broad categories that encompass within them a range of perspectives. They do, however, offer a starting point from which to explore the existing diversity and potential approaches to practice.

Procedural Approach

This approach is based on a view of the world where individuals are seen as objects who fit into a consensus perspective in society (Howe 1987). It has gained considerable credence over the last two decades and considers, in essence, that the function of social work is to contribute to the maintenance of the systems that make up society (Davies 1994). This approach presumes that the nature of service-user problems is rooted in individual actions and decisions, rather than more generally about any injustice inherent in our organisations and institutions. Consequently, those who are not able to, or do not fit within the system are seen as responsible or at fault for their situation, often exhibiting behaviours or actions that are seen as 'abnormal' or 'deviant' (Becker 1963).

The role of the worker in this context is to enable service users to cope with or adopt more 'acceptable' forms of behaviour so that both they and society can benefit from the professional intervention offered. In the main this will be a technical activity that sees the workers' actions as value-free, pragmatic and providing what Dominelli (1998, p. 4) terms 'information about resources and possibilities'. Practice will be concerned with helping and enabling individuals to fit in to society, either for their own benefit or for the greater good. This is not to say that this approach will never challenge or be concerned about the system, but in the main its focus is on individuals fitting the system rather than the system fitting the individual. This is because society itself is seen at best as working positively, at worst as neutral in relation to service users' problems. Consequently, concerns about social justice and anti-oppressive practice will not have a high priority for the worker in this approach. Instead, as Payne (1997, p. 5) points out, it will be about the 'individual's needs'. Relating this to empowerment, this will take place at the level of consumers or customers exercising their rights to complain or exit the service, rather than a democratic interpretation that may seek to challenge the system itself. It is about what Drummond (1993) terms 'first order change': that is, change within the system rather than about the system itself. The procedural approach tends to deal with service users' problems as surface issues, which are observable, rather than as issues having underlying causes. It is consequently more amenable to theories and methods that fit these criteria, particularly those that are able to define, categorise and measure, such as behavouralism or the task-centered method. It is also an approach that tends to place the worker in the role of 'expert', identifying and classifying problems and subsequent solutions.

This approach has a close fit with modern managerial culture and its ethos of dealing with observable issues, measuring and evaluating practice; it is often contained within procedures and codes of practice (Dominelli and Hoogvelt 1996; Watson 2003). This is most apparent in the area of assessment with its growing frameworks of risk and identification of indicators and criteria for appropriate involvement (Pratt 2000). The procedural approach is ultimately concerned about 'what works' and it emphasises short-term and direct intervention. Its attraction for workers is that it provides a degree of certainty about their actions. This is illustrated by the following case study. Like others in the text, we shall return to this case study at various points to illuminate understanding of particular issues.

John's Story

John (aged 84) had resided on his own since the death of his partner six years earlier. He was seen in his local social services office as part of the duty/intake system. It was his sixteenth visit to the office over the previous four months. Every time he had made an appointment it was for help or advice in relation to a practical problem, such as his electricity bill or housing issues. The duty workers' responses on previous occasions were to fix the presenting issue during the appointment and to close contact with John. Despite the high number of contacts, John had never been allocated a social worker, as it was felt that his problems had been resolved. The workers in this situation were responding to John's situation from an approach that considered only presenting problems and getting the job done from an agency and worker perspective – a procedural approach.

His reason for referral on this occasion was to check on whether his insurance policies were effective, as he had recently had a small fire in his home. This was a simple enough task for the worker to deal with as John had the documents with him at the time. By making a few phone calls and writing out a list of outcomes, both John and the worker had a sense of a task completed. Both were satisfied that an appropriate solution had been achieved to a clear and definable 'problem'.

The procedural approach to practice responded to John by locating the presenting problems and providing a quick-fix solution to each as it arose. This sat well with the prevailing norms in the agency, which valued the early resolution of situations, keeping active, open cases to a minimum.

Individual Pathology Approach

This approach focuses on the individual pathology perceived within a given situation that once again is based on a functionalist/consensus view of society (Haralambos et al. 2004). Individuals are seen as subjects rather than objects, who, with appropriate help and counselling, can be enabled to live a more 'healthy' lifestyle. This is an approach with a long history in social work dating back to the 1930s that has come under increasing challenge and scrutiny (Payne 1997). The function of the worker will be to help service users fit more effectively into their families, communities and society. However, to do this means that the worker, through listening to past actions and present problems, needs to enable service users to obtain better explanations and responses than they hold at present

(Dominelli 1998). This approach considers that the root of the service users' difficulties resides in them as individuals and in particular how they have been socialised throughout the lifespan (Bee and Boyd 2003). Whilst there are a wide range of potential responses, in the main they tend to be more concerned with individual pathology and underlying problems rather than with social structure and oppression. Anti-oppressive practice is less frequently given priority, as service users are seen as being 'unhealthy' or 'deviant' and not conforming to the prevailing social norms, rather than account being taken of the wider structural factors. Using this approach with Susan, for example, could lead to an analysis which suggested that her difficulties were rooted in her own poor experiences of being parented rather than the wider issues related to childcare, housing, poverty, etc. (Brooke and Davis 1985).

The role of the worker in this approach is about 'seeking the best possible well being for individuals, groups and communities in society' (Payne 1997, p. 4) in order that they can grow and become self-fulfilled. This is linked to traditional values around respect, self-determination and confidentiality and implies that the worker will facilitate personal growth in the service user. This will be done by utilising a range of skills aimed at enabling the service user to obtain insight or a positive perspective from which to live. The different methods within this approach tend to place the worker in the role of the expert who, in a caring manner, provides the framework for possible solutions to problems, most of which would be about the individual changing his or her behaviour to fit the needs of the wider society.

This approach has not fitted closely with modern managerial culture as it does not easily lend itself to measurement and evaluation. It often has vague and open-ended goals, which can lead to long-term intervention around developing healthy or more appropriate social functioning (Howe 1995). This is not to suggest that it is an uncritical practice; in fact it is the opposite, constantly requiring reflection and consideration of action and activities. Its attraction for workers is that it considers what is going on beneath the surface and therefore can be seen to offer the possibility of 'real' change rather than dealing with the symptoms of the problem, arguably reflecting the difficulties and uncertainty of the real world of the service user (Payne 1997). This offers the possibility of professional development as skills and knowledge need constantly to be worked on and updated. In terms of service users, it is based on similar values to the procedural approach, i.e. individualisation, but is liable to be less congruent in the area of results and clarity of outcomes. This may lead to service users feeling 'irritated' or 'baffled' as workers' intentions are hard to determine or understand (Howe 1987, p. 4).

Looking again at John's situation, it would be possible to construct an understanding that located the 'problem' with him as an individual. Using the individual pathology approach, workers would be likely to look closely at John's response to loss and to develop an analysis that his situation required a more in-depth response. This could mean developing some form of counselling which allowed him to explore his reactions to the death of his partner and to begin to deal with any unresolved issues that remained. The workers' views would be likely to be that John could not move on with his life until he had dealt with these unresolved issues. Erikson's (1963) theory of lifespan development might provide important clues for the worker if she considered him to have become stuck within the final stage of the development process. Intervention would therefore be likely to be seen as taking place over a number of encounters and might not necessarily be what John himself saw as the main focus of his concerns.

This particular worker's approach was based on considering underlying as well as presenting problems. Consequently, she started to talk to John about how he was coping, particularly given his high number of previous visits to the office. What emerged from this brief discussion was that John had lost his sense of purpose as an individual, having few friends and little to keep him occupied during the day. This situation was in direct contrast to his previous working and social life. After discussing the situation with John, the worker agreed with him that his problem was not his insurance policy, but his lack of social networks and how he felt about himself. In an attempt to resolve his loneliness, he had structured his week around visiting agencies, such as the health centre, and social work and housing offices, with different issues, which meant that he had some sense of purpose and was meeting people who were interested in his problems. The worker's response was to talk to John about what services were available to him and whether he wanted to be considered for further intervention.

Working from an individual pathology approach, what became apparent was that there were no quick-fix solutions to John's situation. Rather, what was required was a process of intervention that enabled him to obtain insight into his actions and to develop more effective coping mechanisms. Unlike the previous approach, there is less clarity of purpose and perhaps less sense of 'achievement' in the short term.

Progressive Approach

This approach has also been growing in influence in recent years, particularly within social work education and practice (Lymbery and Butler 2004). In many respects this may be argued to be not an approach but an amalgamation of a number of perspectives that share one common dimension – social justice. In this context the views may share as many differences as similarities. What they have in common is a conflict view of society. However, within the approach it is possible to see the individual as object or subject. The function of social work in this approach is to enable those at the receiving end of oppression to challenge its sources, including the institution of social work and the state (Dominelli 2002a). Service users' situations or problems are in the main less likely to be considered as emanating from their own behaviour or pathology, but are the result of inequalities or unfair power relations that often lead to them being 'victims' rather than the creators of the situation. Consequently, this approach is not about fitting service users to the system, but about empowering them to gain greater awareness of their oppression and to challenge systems.

The role of social work in this approach is to enable those who experience oppression to be able to understand and take more control over their lives (Dominelli 2002a). It is not about workers being 'experts' but rather it is about them using their skills to facilitate change. The 'expert' in terms of this approach would be the service user who knows his/her life and capabilities. The worker's skills and knowledge would be in relation to the system and the ability to create the conditions and support for service users to restructure or exert their power. The worker may be intervening at the micro level of the individual's day-to-day issues and systems, or intervention may be at the more macro level of communities where the worker helps facilitate change. This is not a technical or value-free activity, but one that is undoubtedly based on values and political beliefs about the nature of people and society. This approach is centred on anti-oppressive practice, concerned with 'second order change' – that is, change to the system itself (Drummond 1993), although this does not rule out the possibility of having first order change. This approach, depending on the perspective held, will give greater or lesser emphasis to underlying issues for the service user. Once again, this will depend on the answer to the object/subject question. Therefore consciousness-raising can be about either narrative methods and biography or about political action, or a mixture of both. In this respect it is a critical and constructive practice based on both reflection and action. Relating this to empowerment, we move away from the notion of consumers and customers to that of citizenship; service users are kept informed of what the worker is thinking and why and are enabled to have a say in decisions that impact on their lives (Evans and Harris 2004).

Arguably, one of the key tasks of modern social work is to enable people to make sense of their position vis-á-vis the state. The attraction of this approach for workers resides in the fact that it tries to bridge the gap between the individual and society, thereby potentially recognising all aspects of the person and society (Thompson 1998). In terms of service users, it shares the value base of other approaches in respecting people and their situations. However, results may be less clear depending on the perspective within the approach. It could be claimed that the more overtly political the worker's stance, the more vague and less measurable the work becomes in practice.

Approaching John's situation from a progressive perspective, the worker would need to enter into a dialogue with him in an attempt to establish an understanding of his overall social situation. This would include not only the personal, historical aspects of John's life but also some understanding of his social location within society. It had already been established that John was a prominent local celebrity in his youth thus giving him a status within his community. He was now 84 years old and might, for example, have integrated into his sense of self the many ageist attitudes within his community that might be eroding his self-esteem and confidence. By adopting a biographical method of information-gathering, the worker should be able to learn more about John's understanding of his current situation, based on his own account of his history. Dalrymple and Burke (1995, p. 54) suggest that the development of a genuine partnership takes place over three levels – feelings, ideas and activity. Spending time exploring with John how he saw his life having changed over the years would allow space to acknowledge the relative importance of these events to his coping strategies. By giving him a voice and acknowledging his feelings, he would be able to create a context for past events that allowed the development of ideas for future solutions. He might therefore need to be encouraged to begin truly to articulate his concerns over areas for priority intervention. It would be important for the worker to clarify available options and explain to John his/her perspective on his situation. By being clear with John from the outset about the possible options available and the potential consequences thereof, John would be empowered to make his own decisions about how best to proceed. The worker's role therefore would become one of facilitating and enabling John to develop a clearer understanding of his situation and working with him to create a solution which would be appropriate to him and achievable.

What Kind of Social Worker Do You Want to Be?

As academics, it would be extraordinary if we could enable our students to adopt our favoured approach and to practise from that perspective. However, even if this were desired, it would not be possible as students' knowledge, skills and values and subsequent approach will be personal to them and their experience. This has to be the individual worker's starting point. What we are more realistically concerned about in this book is that workers try to develop an awareness of their approach in order to have a more open and reflective practice that critically and constructively examines what kind of service is being provided. The reason workers need to reflect on their approach is that it determines how they will see themselves as practitioners and in particular how they relate to those using the service. A possible difficulty about reflecting on one's approach is that the different approaches use the same language and concepts, but what they mean in practice can differ significantly. Therefore, when we consider our approach it is important to have an awareness of what is being provided by the worker and experienced by the service user. For example, partnership from a procedural or individual pathology approach would, in the main, include informing service users of what is going to happen, but does not necessarily mean they would have a say over that activity, as the role of the worker – the 'expert' – would be to define the problem and determine the solution. Partnership would mean that the service user was kept informed of intentions and actions. However, partnership from the progressive approach would be to acknowledge the worker's role and authority with the service user and the purpose of the interaction, to establish what was negotiable in that context and then to enable the service user to be part of the problem-identification and problem-solving process. Partnership in this context would be about information sharing and joint decision-making. In both situations we would be using the concept of partnership, but the reality for the service user would be different, as would the skills required of the worker. Therefore, when reflecting on your approach you have to consider many of the words and concepts you use and relate them to what you actually do, rather than to some notion of what you think you do in practice.

Whilst we feel that reflecting on Howe's (1987) question about the individual and society is a helpful starting point in relation to reflecting on our approach, this demands closer examination. Social work practice takes place predominately with individuals who are part of wider social networks. While it is unhelpful to overindividualise situations, so too is it to be overreliant on societal explanations. The following questions are designed to focus your thinking on the key elements of your approach to practice:

- What is the cause of service users' problems – are they personal or structural?

- What is more important, presenting or underlying problems?

- Is your task about helping service users to fit in or about challenging why they are marginalised?

- What is your role – to get things done or to enable those using the service to take more control of their situation?

- Is social work a technical/rational activity or is it based on dealing with uncertainty?

- Who is the expert in your relationship with the service user – you or the service user?

- What is your expertise based on – being a holder of knowledge and skills or being a facilitator?

- Are service users customers or citizens in relation to your work?

You may now want to go back and look at your answers in relation to the three approaches identified above, as these are some of the key areas that distinguish the uniqueness of the different approaches. In particular, they raise the issue of approach to practice, examining whether the worker's favoured approach is reflected in the reality of practice with service users. Often there can be a difference between our espoused position and the actual nature of the work in which we are engaged. This is aptly illustrated by our own experience within social work education. Our intended approach to teaching and learning is progressive, working from a democratic empowerment model. To do this we are aware that we have knowledge that we wish to share with our students and that they have both life and work experiences that can add to this process. Hence we need to find ways of bringing the two together. This requires a process to be developed which enables students to relate their experiences both to the formal learning environment and to future practice in a manner that is participative and interactive. All too often, however, we fall into a didactic way of teaching where we appear as the 'experts' lecturing the students, who appear relatively passive in the process. Having attempted to create an empowering approach that is inclusive, we end up with a very different approach from the one that we intended; one which has the potential to be de-skilling and disempowering to students. We can find many reasons for this. It is easier, it is quicker, we are too busy – all are arguments raised by students about their approach when working with service users in an agency context. It is our view that these are rationalisations rather than reasons. We believe that the social work task should take no longer to complete from a progressive/empowering perspective than from a procedural one. Failure to implement our approach is often a result of our failure to reflect on our actions or to think through the implications of our espoused approach both for ourselves and for service users. Understanding and developing our approach is therefore fundamental to good practice as it underpins every other aspect from assessment through implementation to termination and evaluation.

Practice Theories

When we consider our approach to practice, we are looking at what Coulshed and Orme (1998) term 'grand theories' that explain our understanding of social work as an activity and ultimately influence our work with service users in practice. However, workers also need to be able to utilise what we will term 'middle-level' theories that provide understanding and explanation at a much more direct level of application: that is, theories for practice (Payne 1997; Fook 2002). Workers are faced with a plethora of these middle-level theories, some of which complement and some of which conflict with each other. The difficulty for the worker is that there is little consensus, particularly between the different approaches, about what constitutes acceptable theories for practice. Coulshed and Orme (1998) suggest that to take the 'best' from the range of available theories is the predominant response at present within the practice setting. Whilst we would accept that selecting theory is a personal activity that can allow for considerable scope and flexibility, this will be constrained to some extent by the worker's approach, which will value some types of theory and knowledge over others. If, for example, the worker's approach to practice is individual pathology, he or she is likely to find psychodynamic theories such as attachment and loss helpful in terms of understanding individual service users. This may well be reinforced by the focus of practice within the agency. Whilst there is no definitive list of theories that workers require, the following provides a starting point from which to start thinking about those that underpin our practice.

Theories about society and how it works. This includes theories such as functionalism, conflict theories, feminism and racism. These are theories that add to our understanding about why people and groups behave and react in particular ways within society (Haralambos et al. 2004). Underpinning this are theories of power, who holds it and for what purpose. This should enable workers to start thinking about issues of oppression and strategies for challenging the inappropriate use of power or enabling those disadvantaged in our society to become more powerful (Braye and Preston-Shoot 1995; Dalrymple and Burke 1995).

Theories of poverty and disadvantage. This includes theories that enable workers to reflect on the pervasive impact of lack of resources and social exclusion, how difference is treated and the effects of stigma and alienation. This allows workers to consider strategies which do not blame the individual and which understand the multiple oppressions that race, gender and disability can add to the impact of poverty (Deacon 2002).

Theories of social policy and welfare. This includes theories about the welfare state and its role and purpose in order that workers can develop an understanding of both the organisational and policy context in which they operate and what this means for the services they provide for service users. These would include an appreciation of the importance of the statutory responsibilities of social work practice and how legislation and policy develop from political decision-making (Spicker 1995; Alcock et al. 2003).

Theories of the family and individual development. These enable workers to make sense of the individual stages of human growth and development that impact on the ability of individuals to cope with a range of different life tasks and how they are able to adopt a range of strategies to cope with their lives. In this respect, theories of the family which reflect diversity are important in order that workers can hold a diverse view of living and residing in a multicultural society (Burman 1994; Robinson 1995).

Theories of motivation and change. These look at areas such as organisational and personal change in order that we can reflect on appropriate ways of helping both ourselves and service users to take more control of situations. Such theories provide information about the range of strategies available to both workers and service users to change situations (Lewin 1987; Prochaska et al. 1992).

The purpose of understanding these middle-range theories is to develop an explanation of what is happening in the service user's world and to plan intervention on the basis of that insight.

> For example, if we return to John's situation, it is possible to develop and illuminate our understanding of his general situation by looking at theories about ageism in a society that is based around valuing people in relation to work. John had lost the status he had enjoyed in his working life and he was acutely aware of this fact. In addition, theories of attachment and loss would enable us to have some insight into his present feelings of isolation and loneliness and his need to rectify this by supplementing his declining number of acquaintances and friends with visits to agencies in his area (Howe 1995). However, the problem with these middle-range theories is that they do not fully explain how John himself was feeling about his situation; they only give pointers to the worker about possible explanations. To understand John's situation would require the worker to contextualise his issues within his world and to develop an assessment and intervention strategy based on this understanding.

Therefore, while formal theories should provide a starting point for possible understanding, they need to be incorporated into the service user's own views of the situation and the potential solutions. This point about the limitations of formal theories is made by many social work theorists who argue that they cannot fully explain or understand the world faced by workers and service users (Payne 1997; Parton and O'Byrne 2000; Fook 2002). Such formal theories rarely relate to precise situations, as they do not have the explanatory power to give direct guidance about specific situations for specific service users. Indeed, Parton and O'Byrne (2000) highlight that the danger of these formal theories is that they can be used to label service users, sometimes in a way that does not add anything beyond the ability to categorise and to increase the degree of scrutiny provided by the worker. Whilst the need to describe and categorise may be a legitimate concern for the worker, particularly in relation to statutory work such as child protection or probation, it is rarely the sole focus of the professional worker's task. What then becomes crucial for workers is that, as well as modifying and adapting formal theories, they reflect upon and evaluate their actions to develop their own practice theories. In effect, they are entering into the area of theory-building, which, if appropriate, can be shared with others (Fook 2002). Whilst this is a difficult activity that needs to be systematically structured, this is no reason for workers to avoid developing knowledge and understanding at the direct-practice level. Indeed, if they are to continue to develop their professional status, social work needs to articulate much more clearly its own practice theories rather than adopting wholesale those drawn from other academic disciplines.

The concern that formal theories have limitations in terms of practice should not unduly concern professional practitioners. Social work is not a science in the traditional sense, dealing with certainties and provable facts, but instead is concerned mainly with uncertainty, often around areas of feelings, reflections and opinions. Uncertainty about situations, their causes and potential resolutions is what marks social work as a unique professional activity (Parton and O'Byrne 2000). Consequently, social workers need to develop an understanding of the interrelationship between formal and direct-practice theories and their own experience of what works for them within their own approach. The key to good practice in this context is exploring what specific skill, knowledge or action was effective in enabling service users to make their own sense of that uncertainty and to find ways of making it more acceptable or manageable. This does not necessarily mean that positive change will always be the outcome. It may be about supporting people to live with situations that will not improve or may even get worse. Failing to acknowledge this reality of uncertainty can lead to a formalised hierarchy of knowledge that places formal learning at the pinnacle, leaving learning from experience as much less valued.

Formal theories are a fundamental requirement for the worker in developing good practice. This book looks at methods of intervention in detail, as they can provide a useful way of helping our thinking and understanding and subsequently adding structure and purpose to our work. However, even in relation to methods, their use and applicability is open to challenge and interpretation, particularly when related directly to service users and their situations. This process of distilling formal theories through the filter of experiential learning and practice wisdom is an important means of developing practice theories which are both useful and relevant. In recent years this area has been given more credence by the work of people such as Schön (1987) and Parton and O'Byrne (2000). Our experience, however, is that it still requires considerable development and valuing by lecturers, practice teachers and workers themselves (Watson and West 2003).

Knowledge for Practice

So far we have been concerned about how theories influence our practice. Not every situation, however, is new, requiring workers to construct their understanding of situations from the beginning. Over time, workers develop a knowledge base which reflects their understanding of the realities of social work and social work practice. Through experiences in practice; reflection on how they and others carry out their work; reading the experiences of others and studying research findings, workers develop their understanding of theories for practice. This builds into a knowledge base which can be drawn upon 'so that we are not reinventing the wheel every time we act' (Thompson 2000, p. 51). Knowledge in this respect is constantly developing and evolving to meet the changing needs of the practice context, providing a pool on which to draw and guide both understanding and actions. The knowledge base which workers require continues to expand and it is unrealistic to think that any one worker can possess all the knowledge that he or she is ever likely to need. What is important is that workers be aware of what knowledge they hold and how to find out what they may additionally require. There are, however, areas of knowledge which are important for workers to develop.

The first of these and the main focus of this chapter is the approach to practice. As we have previously discussed, knowledge of our approach becomes knowledge of ourselves and how we are practising. While we would not wish to suggest that workers need to subject themselves to a form of analysis, it is important that they should be attuned to their own contribution to relationships. The problem with self-knowledge, however, is that it is one of the most difficult forms of knowledge to be sure of and the one most liable to change, depending on circumstances. That said, it is key knowledge for workers, as it determines what are seen as the problems or issues and potentially determines the solutions.

The second area of knowledge which is important is what works, when, for whom and why. In essence, this is also a continuation of self-knowledge, as workers will also be drawing on their own experiences of what works for them. By developing an understanding of current research, workers are able to draw upon the collective wisdom of others rather than simply relying upon personal experience. This concern with 'what works' is an area of growing importance in the present managerial climate. Our concern, however, is that workers need to move beyond the tangible and easily identified also to evaluate what improves the lives of those they are working with and why. A good example of what we mean by this is provided by Bullock et al. (1998) who, by researching workers' and families' experiences, were able to identify what would be successful practice in the very difficult and complex task of children leaving care to return home. This is not to argue that all workers need to keep abreast of every twist and turn in practice and research, but it is a fundamental requirement to be aware of important developments and use this knowledge to enhance practice (Frost 2002).

The third area of knowledge that we consider crucial for workers in developing good practice is that of the agency, its decision-making structure, and policies and procedures. Social work as an organisational activity has in recent years become more proceduralised, with clear lines of accountability (Watson 2002). To continue to develop professional practice in this managerial climate, workers need to have knowledge of the organisation, how and why decisions are made and what is expected of them in given situations. In effect, they need to be aware of their role and function within the organisation and what this means for professional autonomy and discretion (Clegg 1990). It is only by understanding how the organisation functions both formally and informally that social workers are going to be able to get the best out of the organisation, rather than being controlled and limited in their actions. This may seem a strange statement to make, but knowledgeable workers in this area are not just managed by their organisation, but also manage the organisation. This can occur because whilst many of the procedures and decision-making structures tend to be concerned with rationing resources, particularly the workers' time, they are usually presented in more progressive terms such as good practice or partnership in any policy documentation (Postle 2002). Knowledgeable workers are able to use this understanding to advocate on their own and on the service users' behalf to obtain the resources or conditions to develop good practice.

As we shall explore in subsequent chapters, approaches to practice underpin all other aspects of the social work task. It is, therefore, vital that workers develop a clear, critical awareness of their chosen approach and how this in turn influences the process of assessment, the selection of method and the subsequent evaluation (see Figure 2.1).

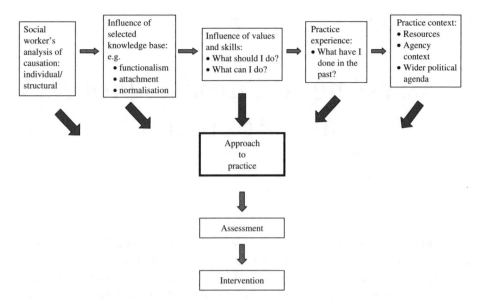

Figure 2.1 Developing an Approach to Social Work Practice

Summary of Chapter

1. Effective practice requires workers to develop a conscious awareness of their approach.

2. The worker's orientation to the task will draw upon a number of aspects including an understanding of society and how it works; an awareness of wider political issues; personal and professional values; current knowledge base and organisational and cultural aspects of the agency.

3. There are three broad categories of approach to practice: procedural, individual pathology and progressive. Each has its own unique response to service users and will in turn affect the processes of assessment, implementation, termination and evaluation.

4. Developing an approach to practice assists workers to develop a clear sense of their own professional persona and the skills they require in order to be effective. In this context, theory for practice is as important as understanding grand and middle-range theories. It will be influenced by the worker's approach, an awareness of what is effective and a clear understanding of the organisational context in which the work occurs.

3

Assessment: Purpose, Process and Approach

Assessment is at the heart of all good social work practice. It covers a spectrum of activities, from observation and judgments made within the context of an initial encounter through to more formal and complex frameworks of assessment. Its purpose is to enhance understanding of the service user's situation, helping workers to identify areas for potential change that will assist the development of a rationale for future intervention. In this respect, assessment and how it is carried out will be influenced by a number of factors, including who initiated the request, the nature of the prevailing concerns, the agency's policies and procedures and, last but not least, the worker's approach. This latter area will influence not only what is considered important in the service users' situation but also how they might contribute to the assessment process. Effective assessment needs workers to balance a number of competing and often conflicting demands in order that they obtain an understanding of service users and their situation.

Assessment is also a process that has a number of stages, which can arguably be identified even if they do not always occur in the logical manner (Lloyd and Taylor 1995; Coulshed and Orme 1998). The stages of assessment are:

● preparing for meeting the service user;

● meeting the service user to build a relationship and obtain relevant information;

● reflecting on and analysing the information gathered about the service user to determine the appropriate action to be followed;

● implementation of action.

Each of these stages raises issues and dilemmas for the worker to resolve in relation to completing their assessment. In relation to *preparing for meeting the service user*, this stage involves the worker having to determine what information needs to be gathered in relation to the service user prior to any meeting. Obvious sources of information include agency case files, other agencies' and professionals' records/reports and the often overlooked sources of relatives, friends and neighbours. In this situation, workers often need to decide how much information, if any, to utilise. This activity will directly impact on complex issues of confidentiality and empowerment on the workers' part, as they try to obtain a balance between preparing themselves for the assessment and pre-empting future actions on their and the service user's part. However, it is an issue that has to be addressed as, at a practical level, failure to obtain appropriate information could leave the worker entering particularly difficult circumstances without being adequately prepared. For example, not reviewing existing information might mean that the worker would not have considered from both his/her and the service user's perspectives the most appropriate place to meet. This could potentially put the worker at risk if the service user had been violent to social workers in the past. This is a real issue, given the growing number of recorded incidents of violence towards social workers in recent years (Spencer and Munch 2003). From the service users' perspective, lack of consideration of previous contacts also mean that they have repeatedly to go over their situation to new workers, which can be stressful or cause unnecessary distress. Holding appropriate information means that workers do not have to pry into the service user's life but can confirm that they have an understanding of past events and work. However, too much information is also problematic, as it can lead to the worker forming a judgment about the service user solely based on others' experiences (Coulshed and Orme 1998). This can lead to confirming other workers' assessments, despite the changes that have occurred in the service user's situation in the meantime. What is required is for the worker to retain a healthy scepticism about others' information without losing sight of the possibilities and lessons it can afford. Obtaining this balance is something that comes with ongoing reflection and learning. Our opinion on this matter is that it is better for students and new workers to err on the side of caution. As long as workers are able to reflect critically on how they have been influenced by external bias, then it is better to have too much information rather than too little until they have confidence in their assessment skills.

Meeting the service users entails consideration of from whom workers should seek information beyond the direct service user. All too often workers focus on the immediate service user, who, whilst important, may not hold all the relevant information on the situation being assessed. This occurs when an approach has been adopted that individualises problems, often to the detriment and disempowerment of the service user involved in the assessment. Good assessment entails gathering information from a variety of sources (including family, friends and other agencies) and checking out the currency and accuracy of such information by a process of cross-referencing in order to reach a valid conclusion. This raises questions about confidentiality and service users' permission to seek information about their circumstances. Working in partnership would suggest that as far as possible these issues should be discussed with service users and their agreement sought. However, this may not always be possible if we are assessing situations where danger or harm may exist. Gathering information also means we have to consider what information is appropriate for this assessment and situation. Assessment is not about gathering every possible piece of information and then making a judgement, it is about obtaining *relevant* information (Scottish Office 1997). Service users, no matter who they are, have rights to their personal thoughts and feelings as well as their privacy, and workers must ensure that they do not abuse their position by violating such rights (Banks 2004). Good assessment means repeatedly questioning what information is needed in a situation and why. For example, information about John's past life was relevant because it helped us understand why he felt isolated and lonely. Determining the level of information required is a difficult balancing act for the worker to achieve. However, if we are to provide a service that is based around service users as partners, we need to work at it. In trying to achieve this balance, it is important that we should consider more than the presenting problem. For an appropriate assessment to be carried out, it is essential to consider all the factors relevant to the person's life, including thoughts and feelings.

Reflecting and analysing is a skilled activity that is best done with the service user, as it provides context and relevance to the information that is being assessed. The relevance of any assessment rests in the workers' (and service users') ability to sift and analyse the information that they have obtained, in order to make sense of the service users' situation and ensure that future intervention is appropriate to their needs and capabilities (Milner and O'Byrne 2002). This skill has increasingly been neglected in practice in recent years as social work has become more proceduralised and decisions about services and resources have become the preserve of first-line and middle managers (Dominelli and Hoogevelt 1996). Empowering practice is about more than gathering information for managers, it is also about workers making judgements around their understanding and knowledge, determining with the service user what is relevant and to what end – it is about making decisions. Therefore, assessment, if is to be meaningful, requires workers to develop an analysis of the available information as a springboard for future action (O'Sullivan 1999). Parker and Bradley (2003, p. 39) provide a range of 'tools and diagrammatical aids' to assist with this process. They include the use of culturagrams that in the context of anti-oppressive practice are a more useful means of understanding complex family networks.

Action forms the final stage in the assessment process. This requires workers to draw up a plan of action and to evaluate its effectiveness. In reality this is not as precise an activity as one might imagine. Service users rarely follow a sequential process of assessment, providing information in the order that workers would desire. Life is rarely like that; people tell their story in their own unique way. This means that workers may have to take action before they have gathered or sifted all the information they would have desired. The implication of this is that workers invariably make assessments around partial information, including thoughts and feelings about a situation. Given the uncertainty that characterises these areas and processes, it is crucial that conclusions remain open to review and evaluation in the light of changing circumstances and information. None the less, this should not deter workers from being clear about their role and purpose and thereby providing a baseline for evaluation of the impact of any intervention. Professional social work requires appropriate assessments leading to effective interventions. It is only by doing this that an understanding can be developed of what works for and with service users rather than relying on folklore and intuition (Thompson 2000).

In recent years the importance of assessment has grown for both social workers and case managers as agencies have been increasingly faced with matching limited resources to what would appear limitless need. Consequently, agencies have had to find ways of making decisions about whether they should provide a service or not. In this respect, assessment has become a crucial tool in screening referrals for resources, including those of the social workers themselves. This can involve evaluating the referral against pre-existing eligibility criteria. On the assumption that the information gathered does enable a service to be provided, the function of the assessment should then be to develop an understanding about the best form of intervention to meet the needs of the service user. Assessment is about establishing the targets for and objectives of intervention, giving reasons for taking or not taking action and consequently providing a baseline for evaluating future practice. By asking basic questions such as:

● what needs to be changed;

● how this will be achieved, given the service users' capabilities; and

● whether the worker/agency will be able to support the intervention,

workers should be able to describe what is going on, offer possible explanations and prescribe possible interventions. Therefore, whilst assessment may be an outcome in itself rather than part of a wider process, it is in many instances the beginning of the social work process with service users. Consequently, social work assessments need to be flexible enough to accommodate the unexpected, whilst structured enough to enable both service user and worker to understand what is being undertaken and how it will be achieved. As Lloyd and Taylor (1995, p. 699) succinctly put it, 'social work assessment is not a static, once-and-for-all process whereby the worker arrives at the definitive "right" answer. Assessment is ongoing throughout the contact, and it is a dynamic process in which the worker, service user, agency (or agencies) and other interested parties are all involved and affect the outcome.'

Despite this awareness that assessment is an ongoing activity, the reality of practice for many workers is that it becomes a one-off event which is used to confirm our initial concerns throughout the period of intervention (Milner and O'Byrne 2002). This often occurs because ongoing assessment, by implication, requires critical reflection on practice and an ongoing review of actions that challenges the workers' own skills and understanding. However, failure to carry out this task means that workers may not utilise the growing level of understanding of service users as their relationship develops over time. It also fails to recognise that service users, because of their past experience or present knowledge of the social services, may have concerns or suspicions about information that they should pass on to the worker. This suspicion is understandable in terms of people rightly protecting their information, thoughts and feelings from strangers until such time as they have developed a degree of trust. Consequently, it would be unrealistic to expect service users to provide a full and total account of their lives to a stranger who is working from a position of authority. A more realistic stance would be to expect service users to give what information they feel is necessary to cover the present situation. This would suggest, therefore, that as the relationship develops between the worker and service user, more relevant information should potentially become available for consideration. This notion of relevant information being built up over time can be seen in relation to Brian's situation.

Brian

Brian, aged 27, had been convicted of assault following a fight with three other men after a local football match. All had been drinking heavily and the police charged all four with assault as each made statements incriminating the others. Brian had a history of violent offences, usually while under the influence of alcohol. He had been unemployed for the previous three years, having lost his last job because he had frequently arrived at work under the influence of alcohol. He lived with his parents but they were 'fed up with his behaviour' and had asked him to move out unless he sought help with his excessive drinking. The outcome of this additional conviction meant that Brian was placed on probation. Initially Brian was reticent to provide the full details of his drinking habit to the allocated worker, holding back on the frequency and level of alcohol consumption and what this meant for his behaviour. However, after approximately six meetings he felt able to open up about his alcohol consumption to the worker, whom he now felt he could trust. This had implications for the initial assessment of Brian's situation, which had touched upon concerns in this area but had not been able to explore them owing to Brian's reluctance to consider his alcohol consumption as a problem. In the light of the new information provided by Brian about his situation, it became clear to the worker that specialised support needed to be arranged to help him to reduce his alcohol consumption. This enabled Brian to take the positive steps he desired, such as stopping offending and obtaining employment and his own accommodation. Therefore, to limit assessment to the initial stage of involvement in situations such as Brian's ignores the fact that it is a continuous process where internal and external factors continue to affect our ability to obtain a full and accurate picture.

In terms of the social work process, assessment is usually the first stage in building a relationship between the service user and social worker/agency. This is true whether the assessment is to determine what ongoing support social workers can offer or is the initial stage of care management. First impressions and experiences are crucial, as they often shape and influence both workers' and service users' future responses (Milner and O'Byrne 2002). It is important, therefore, for workers to be able to use this experience in an empowering way that includes the service user and ensures that his/her needs are met in the most appropriate manner. Unless this occurs, workers may be failing to meet the service users' needs and wasting precious resources including their own and the service users' time. Worse still, they may disempower and alienate the service users to such an extent that any future intervention will be less liable to succeed, as they rightly feel that they have not been listened to and that their needs have been ignored. Consequently, good practice in assessment should be a partnership between the worker and service user, where those receiving the service are enabled to understand and be part of the process (Dalrymple and Burke 1995).

The changing nature of assessment in recent years away from need to risk is a cause for concern as it moves the aim of assessment away from a more holistic stance of the person and their situation to one particular aspect – risk (Parton 1996). Risk is important, but overemphasis on this one area means that workers are liable to fail to understand the service users' situation and may inappropriately target resources. It also has the potential to shift the focus of assessment away from what can be done – building on the positive – to what should be avoided – emphasising the negative. What is required is a balance between these activities, reflecting who the service users really are and what they are capable of doing to change their lives. This has come under challenge within the present managerial ethos, impacting upon and influencing social work. Assessment is increasingly being seen as a mechanistic, technical activity that can be broken down into discrete tasks carried out by unqualified staff (Watson 2002). Whilst assessment is not the sole preserve of the qualified worker, good assessment is a skilled activity that requires appropriate training and understanding if it is to be carried out effectively. Whilst assessments may be routine, there is no guarantee of this being the case and, in our view, agencies should be using their most skilled staff in this area, ensuring that service users needs are fully assessed and agencies can appropriately prioritise resources.

Assessment: Risk and Partnership

In recent years the process of assessment has become increasingly more difficult and skilled, particularly as a result of government and professional expectations around two key areas: risk and partnership. Defining risk in relation to social work practice has obtained increasing currency. As Kelly (1996) points out, one of the reasons for this is that workers often have to work with people of whom they have little knowledge at the time of intervention. This situation means that, even with the best available information, the worker is liable to be limited in his/her ability to determine the best possible action. The aim of risk assessment in this context is to enable workers to gauge the potential danger and then to take remedial action if they are concerned about the potential consequences. In relation to the assessment process, risk has generated a plethora of assessment frameworks and checklists which, if completed, are believed to indicate the level of risk (DoH 2000; McIvor et al. 2001). Parton (1996), however, cautions against this notion of implying certainty, arguing that risk assessment is part of a move towards targeting groups and, in particular, those who are affected by poverty or oppression. In this respect he suggests that risk assessment may not necessarily be a positive activity, given its limited predictive potential. In essence, risk-assessment frameworks may give the illusion of being scientific and objective, but as yet they fall far short of this as the indicators are at best limited in their predictability.

Risk and need are not the same thing and what this means for service allocation is that many service users, despite their needs, may not obtain a service in modern social work with its resource limitations. This has led Lloyd and Taylor (1995) to conclude that while risk assessment should be a component of the process it is not be the sole focus of the assessment, which should be a balance between concerns, strengths, risks, needs, rights and resources. Counter to this is the view that risk assessment provides a framework to make concerns explicit in relation to a particular situation, thereby enabling open and transparent discussion about what is of concern and how this can be managed. To this end social work has increasingly moved into the area of interdisciplinary work and shared assessment (Bradley and Manthorpe 2000).

To undertake a risk assessment implies that we have some notion of what risk itself is and what this means for the situation. Whilst there is much debate about the concept, Brearley's (1982) definition, despite its limitations, continues to be relevant by providing a working framework for moving forward. He suggests that risk is the possibility of a present or future event involving possible negative outcomes, usually associated with loss, damage or harm. In effect, risk assessment becomes a decision based round uncertainty and unpredictability that is calculated in relation to the given knowledge that the worker and service user are able to bring forward at that point in time. However, risk is more than just the possibility that loss, damage or harm may occur. It also has to be considered in relation to the possible consequences of that event. Therefore, not all risky situations will be concerning to workers. This could be seen in John's situation, where he was at real risk not only of becoming socially isolated but also, as an older person, of suffering declining physical and mental health. In our ageist society, however, these real risks may not be translated into concerns for workers. They are often seen as inevitable, an attitude that would never be accepted in areas such as child care.

Given the plethora of frameworks for assessing risk, Brearley's (1982) work is still helpful because it identifies and provides a framework for assessing risk that can be debated and discussed between practitioner, service user and agency. This framework makes the distinction between general predictive hazards and situational hazards, identifying that not all factors are of equal importance in terms of risk. General predictive hazards are usually linked to background factors that have been important in a person's life and may be indicative but are not prescriptive. Any attempt totally to eliminate the risk would need those background hazards to be remedied. In the short term, however, workers may only be able to seek out ways of minimising or securing protection around these areas of risk. Situational hazards tend to be those in the present environment that are causing concern and are those that workers may seek to minimise or alleviate. Brearley's framework also offers a starting point from which to develop ways of reviewing and thinking about risk itself. He argues that when assessing risk factors in any situation, workers should not concentrate solely on the hazards but should also value the strengths that the service user and the worker can bring to any situation as a means of minimising the potential dangers. This framework is in essence rather like a SWOT analysis where Strengths, Weaknesses, Opportunities and Threats can be examined as axes on a grid, diagrammatically presenting relevant information. It promotes thinking about what would be the anticipated outcome, given the strengths and potential opportunities of the service user, while acknowledging the threats and concerns in relation to a situation. Assessing risk requires a realistic appraisal of what change is possible, which situational hazards can be worked with and when the background hazards can be addressed. In these situations it might well be that the worker's role will change from being one of a change agent to someone who is clearly monitoring or controlling the situation. While for many workers this may not be the most comfortable situation, it is likely to be their role in a risk-assessment situation. Finally, Parton (1985) makes a crucial point that the price of having *risky* people in the community is eternal vigilance. What this implies is that risk assessment is something that cannot just be done on an occasional ad hoc reactive basis but needs to be a proactive, planned activity that is constantly clear about its aims and goals.

Frameworks for risk assessment are still at an early stage of development. Concerns have been expressed about the potential for models of assessment to be utilised that imply a degree of expertise which they do not merit in practice (Beaumont 1999). However, the claim that it is scientific and requires the skills of an expert has tended to mean that service users have been excluded from the process. Risk assessment, however, has the potential to be used within a more democratic model of assessment where concerns and consequences are openly discussed with service users, who are able to make informed choices about their lives.

The process of assessment has also been influenced in recent years by the emerging importance of the concept of partnership. Whilst this is not a new concept, what is now different is the growing importance, in government guidance and legislation, of partnership with service users (Smale et al. 1993). The problem with this guidance is that partnership is rarely defined and can therefore be interpreted in a variety of ways. Of concern is that working in partnership can become a practice that workers utilise at the minimal level of informing rather than working directly with service users. Partnership as Dalrymple and Burke (1995, p. 64) point out is more than informing. It is about the 'notion that service users and providers should be included as far as possible as fellow citizens in the decision-making process that affects their lives'. What partnership does not mean is that the worker and service user are equal in terms of their relationship. It is doubtful, given the structural difference and power differentials between the worker and service user, that this level of equality could ever occur. The purpose of partnership is as far as possible to remove artificial barriers to the relationship with those using the service. It should be an attempt to transform the power held by service users in order that they can take more control over their lives. This moves the focus of the service from being provider-led to service-user-led. Partnership is about a process of working that enables service users to have the knowledge and confidence to take more control over the issues effecting and affecting their situation. It is about trying to enable them to become more powerful. This is a negotiated and evolving process.

Transforming power requires two vital ingredients according to Braye and Preston-Shoot (1995): sufficient information to understand and take part, and the ability to influence decisions. Unless these are achieved, it is about consultation or participation rather than partnership. To achieve partnership, workers will need to give consideration in both the assessment and implementation processes to how they can enable service users to become more confident. Workers need to assist service users to develop their skills and help to remove any barriers in the decision-making processes. As Healy (2000) points out, partnership may be about the big issues of organisational decision-making, but it is also about the everyday actions as workers. A practical example of this in relation to assessment is provided by Thompson (2000, p. 137) who states that partnership is about the workers setting out their stall: 'Making it clear at the beginning of our involvement why we are there, what our role is, what we expect of them, what they can expect from us and so on.' It is in this context that partnership can be most real, but is also significantly underutilised, as workers hold on to their power at the expense of the service user. Looking back for a moment at Susan's situation, a partnership approach to the assessment of her child-care needs would acknowledge her skill and knowledge as a parent in choosing a suitable resource rather than the worker adopting the role of 'expert' gatekeeper of scarce resources.

Arguably, the concepts of risk and partnership, which are an integral part of the assessment process, are conflicting rather than complementary in their effect. Risk tends to move power and expertise into the workers' or agencies' domain. Partnership moves power away from these sources towards the service user. Our contention is that they need not be conflicting, but that workers and agencies may find it less threatening to give emphasis to risk rather than to develop an approach based on partnership. Whilst as concepts these are continually evolving, risk has obtained greater applicability in practice as it tends not to challenge workers and indeed may serve to protect them from external pressures. Partnership, on the other hand, can be threatening as service users become more powerful and may challenge not only the system but also the worker. What is required is not that we ignore risk, but rather that we begin to locate it in an open framework that enables service users to be part of the process of assessment. Whilst this may be problematic, better decisions about risk will be made as a result. In this context, risk and partnership can become complementary, leading to risk assessments that are both informed by and determined by service-user involvement. This is likely to move risk assessment away from a negative activity to one that has the potential to empower service users.

How Models of Assessment Influence Approach

Assessment is not a technical, value-free or mechanistic activity that can be rigidly followed. It is an activity that will be influenced by both the service users' situation and the workers' approach. In particular, the workers' approach and the relative importance they give to activities such as risk and partnership will influence what they perceive as important and how they go about gathering information. In relation to this latter area, how we gather information, Smale et al. (1993) identify three different models of assessment. These are the *questioning, procedural* and *exchange* models, all of which approach the assessment process in different ways.

The *questioning* model is based on workers using set questions to gather information from 'passive' service users. The worker assumes the role of the expert who is able to interpret and define the data in relation to the service users' needs. In many respects this model fits the traditional expert model of professionalism in that the person who holds the power is the worker who has the ability to define the service users' problems. According to Smale et al. (1993), this model is probably most relevant for workers in relation to risk assessment. It is a model that limits and restricts the involvement of the service user and should therefore, in terms of an empowering approach to practice, have limited application. That is not to say that workers do not need to gather information, but that the gathering of information is not the sole purpose of the social work assessment or intervention.

The *procedural* model is based around completing guidelines or checklists to establish whether service users fit agency criteria for services. The expert in this model is the person who has designed the forms, the worker's role being to gather information from service users. Smale et al. (1993) believe there is a tendency for this model to be used in community care assessments, as they are subject to resource constraints. While this may or may not be true, it is clear that the procedural model has a number of strengths and limitations. Workers do have to gather information for agency purposes and, as a consequence, require both factual and subjective information to complete resource applications. However, the danger with this procedural model, as with the questioning model, is that the basic social-work value of respecting persons and their thoughts and feelings can become secondary to the information-gathering process. This can particularly be the case if workers adopt an indiscriminate approach to gathering information from service users. In doing this, they are then able to claim that they have covered all the bases in relation to issues such as risk.

The *exchange* model is based on the premise that service users are experts in their own lives and situations. Consequently, the relationship between the worker and the service user should be one where the worker enables the service user to identify strengths and resources as well as weaknesses and limitations. This enables and empowers service users to take more control over the assessment process and how they will be involved in the resolution of any difficulties and dilemmas. The model is not about ignoring the issues of power and empowerment, but about having these transparent and explicit in relation to the service user in order that they can make decisions effectively and influence their own lives.

What can be drawn from these models is that they can all use the same assessment framework, but to different effect. The questioning and procedural models place the worker's or agency's needs at the heart of the process; the exchange model focuses on the service user. They also have different interpretations of expertise in the situation and what this means for the role of the service user and social worker. The exchange model identifies the service user as the expert and the worker facilitates this expertise. The questioning model identifies the worker as the expert and the service user as a relatively passive player in this process. The procedural model almost replicates this process, although the worker's role will become less skilled. Whilst workers may need to hold some skills in all three models, as they will be required to ask questions and complete forms, Smale et al. (1993, p. 22) state, 'it should be clear that some dimensions of each exclude the application of others'. It is important to be clear about whose purpose is served by the assessment and who holds the power to determine its reality. In effect, these models replicate the concerns expressed in the three approaches identified in Chapter 2. Whilst offering a crude comparison, it would be possible to relate these models to the approaches to practice. The questioning model could be seen as reflecting the concerns and stance of the individual pathology approach, where expertise is located in the workers' role and their ability to determine problems and solutions. The procedural model, that of the maintenance approach, assumes that workers will make the system work efficiently by fulfilling its requirements. The exchange model, utilising the progressive approach, has as its concern working in partnership with service users who have expertise about their lives.

The differences between these models and their underpinning approach in practice can be seen in relation to Sandeep and Ravinder's situation. Sandeep (39) had recently been involved in an accident that had left him paralysed from the waist down. He was still in hospital at the time of the referral to social services but had reached a stage where medical staff considered he was ready for discharge. Sandeep was married and had two sons aged 9 and 14. His wife, Ravinder (31) spoke very little English but had indicated to Sandeep that she did not feel confident about her ability to cope with the demands of the boys and his needs. She had been treated for depression some two years earlier and feared a return of this condition if she were placed under stress. The family lived in a small terraced house which had two bedrooms and a bathroom upstairs and a sitting room, kitchen and small bedroom downstairs. The downstairs bedroom had until recently been a dining room but was converted to give the two boys their own bedrooms. The house had a large back garden that gave access to the rear of the house. The front of the house was reached via eight stone steps. Tarjinder, the younger son, was finding it very difficult to accept what had happened to his father and tried to get out of visiting him in hospital whenever he could. Tarjinder's behaviour at school was giving cause for concern and he had been truanting. The school had contacted the family and the social services about these concerns.

Approaching this situation using a questioning model of assessment the worker would concentrate on gathering as much information as possible about the situation, concentrating on the practicalities and potential solutions. In this respect, the concerns for the worker would concentrate on the risks to Sandeep's return, such as Ravinder's depression and Tarjinder's behaviour. The resolution to the problem might be for the worker to identify and work with the family on how these risks could be minimised, potentially reflecting an approach that focused on the obvious negative aspects of the situation and how these could be alleviated. The expectation of the family would be to provide the information that the worker sought, without influencing the process of what was being gathered and to what effect. Using a procedural approach, the worker would also set the agenda for the assessment, ensuring that the information the agency was looking for was provided in order that appropriate resources could be obtained. What is unlikely in both these models is that the family's own understanding of the situation would be explored, as this would not necessarily be central to the worker's agenda for the assessment. Such an approach might serve to confirm existing oppression and racism felt by the family. Alternatively, using an exchange model, the starting point for the worker would be to explore what the situation meant for the family and to enable them to make decisions about their future, exploring how the workers and the agency could, if possible, support the process. In this context, for example, the issue of Ravinder's depression might assume much less significance, as she put her own perspective on her health. As Fernando (1995) has noted, what is perceived by predominantly white mental health professionals as depression is often a means of coping with endemic racism. In addition, the family would also have the opportunity to explain and develop what importance issues such as ethnicity had in their situation, rather than this issue being ignored or the impact assumed. Therefore, whilst all three models of assessment would start off with the same information, how the assessment developed would influence what that meant. How empowered the family were in the process might vary considerably.

What these models do is raise the question of how workers are approaching the assessment process. It is our contention that although the questioning and procedural models will fit with the managerial agenda, they are not as consistent with an empowering agenda that is based on partnership. Our concern is that too many assessments fall into the questioning or procedural models, with workers only gathering information as this fits an agenda of getting the job done, often under severe resource constraints. This practice is often justified as being a practical response to large workloads. This can lead to the marginalisation of service users where promoting their contribution to the assessment process is seen as time-consuming. The concern tacitly held by workers utilising such models appears to be that working in partnership will alter the balance of power in the relationship, thereby changing the workers' ability to maintain control over their workload. Whilst gathering information is a key part of assessment, how this is done should reflect the needs and capabilities not just of the worker but also of the service user. It is our contention that ethical assessment – based on exchange – is arguably no more time-consuming than questioning and procedural models, but may be more skilled and challenging to carry out. The difference between the models is based not on additional work but on the level of honesty and openness employed by the worker. The implication of being open is that workers may have to face questions about their values and how consistent these are with an empowering anti-oppressive practice. In this context Dalrymple and Burke (1995, p. 120) provide a framework that can inform good practice in the area of assessment:

1 Assessment should involve those being assessed.

2 Openness and honesty should permeate the process.

3 Assessment should involve the sharing of values and concerns.

4 There should be acknowledgement of the structural context of the process.

5 The process should be about questioning the basis of the reason for proposed action and all those involved should consider alternative courses of action.

6 Assessment should incorporate the different perspectives of the people involved.

When considering assessment from an empowering anti-oppressive perspective, it is a much more complex process than the simple asking of questions designed to obtain formulaic answers. It is a skilled activity that requires reflective practice to ensure that empowering relationships are at the heart of the process (Lloyd and Taylor 1995).

Assessment Skills: Communication, Negotiation and Decision-Making

To carry out an assessment that is accurate and empowering, workers need to develop a range of skills. The skills of communication, negotiation and decision-making are central to this process as they lay the basis of relating to, working alongside and agreeing the appropriate direction. Effective communication is required in order to help put people at ease, gather information and enable and empower service users to feel part of the social work process (Lishman 1994; Thompson 2002). Therefore, failure to communicate effectively can all too often lead to service users being confused about what is expected of them or failing to understand the reason for social work intervention. Consequently, to work in partnership and empower service users it is important to communicate with them in a way that those using the service can understand and can build upon. This is of paramount importance when assessing and working with service users from ethnic minorities, who, according to Thompson (1997), need to be listened to very carefully to ensure that we do not impose our own interpretation on their communication. This is equally true in relation to areas such as gender, class, age and disability, all of which can impact on the type and style of communication which we use and deem appropriate.

Communication is an area of social work practice that has obtained considerable attention in recent years and is covered in most textbooks. On reviewing the literature there are a number of areas of communication that can and do influence the social work relationship. These are:

● verbal

● non-verbal

- paraverbal

- written

When we consider these areas we are not just thinking of the worker, but also of the service user's contribution to the relationship. Communication between workers and service users, therefore, does not take place in a vacuum. It has a purpose, which in terms of assessment is to gather information to come to a conclusion about what needs to be done, if anything. What this means is that both parties will enter that relationship with preconceptions and agendas that will influence how and what is communicated, both verbally and non-verbally. In Susan's situation, for example, both she and the worker are likely to come to their meeting with preconceived ideas of what constitutes 'good parenting'. Each will be looking for cues – verbal, paraverbal and non-verbal – to support their world-view. What workers need to be aware of is that for many service users this will be a traumatic or anxiety-provoking experience that may impact on their contribution and way of communicating. It is important, therefore, that workers enable service users to feel that they are respected and that their contribution is valued early on in the relationship, thereby enabling them to get past the concerns they have about social work involvement and to move on to actively engaging, observing and listening to what is happening in the interview setting. 'Active listening', as described by Lishman (1994), is a special alertness on the part of the listener, where the aim is to listen closely to the details of the service user.

Verbal communication, as Thompson (2002, p. 87) points out, 'has two elements: what is said and what is heard – the output and the input'. In relation to what is said, workers should set the tone for interview by being clear about their purpose and what they expect from the service user during the meeting, reassuring them that their contribution will be valued. To do this needs workers to ask and answer questions, and engage with and listen to what the service user has to say. Lishman (1994) identifies the key skills in this activity as questioning, reflecting, focusing, summarising, confronting and challenging. These are used to obtain appropriate facts and feeling from the service users and to enable them to develop issues or their understanding of the situation. This is a difficult skill for students and new workers to acquire as it involves a continual judgement about what is appropriate to do at any given point in time, each choice having the potential to stifle as to well as to enhance communication. Too many questions, for example, can give the service user the feeling of being put on the spot; too few questions may mean the interview can drift into an unstructured conversation. Inappropriate confrontation or challenging, particularly early on in the interview, can be perceived as aggressive or hostile; too little challenging means issues may only be seen at face value as they have not been explored in depth (Lishman 1994). The key to this activity and ensuring that it is an empowering experience is to give as much time to the service users' agenda as to your own. They should be the main focus of the interview and this is not possible if the bulk of the talking is done by the worker rather than by the service user. This is where active listening becomes important. Service users should be aware that workers have appropriately heard and acknowledged what they have said, and have reflected on their statements to ensure that their interpretation of events is confirmed and understood. This verbal communication is a difficult skill which the worker can only build up over time using both critical reflection and supervision.

Communication is not just confined to the spoken word. Non-verbal and paraverbal communication are also important. Non-verbal communication is contained in our posture, gestures, expressions and actions. Paraverbal communication could be described as the short vocal interjections that help maintain the flow of a conversation. The 'uh uh', 'hmm' or short sigh can signify far more than many sentences! A misplaced sigh or inappropriate gesture can complicate the dynamics of that first encounter. These activities can give clues and cues to what people are feeling during the interview. Workers should be looking to consider how consistent these actions are with the verbal in order to help them to think of how they should respond. A simple example could be in relation to a person who is physically displaying his or her discomfort about a situation, but is saying that he or she has dealt with this issue. In this situation the worker might wish to reflect on this fact in order that the issue might be more fully explored. The problem with such communication is that it is more open to misinterpretation than verbal communication, as we draw the wrong conclusions from what we observe. This is much more probable when working with service users from diverse backgrounds, where different customs and practices are liable to pertain. There are also some concerns about the use of such forms of communication in terms of child protection investigations where 'coaching' of children is perceived to occur when they provide responses that are thought to be required by the adults concerned (Clyde 1992). Finally non-verbal and paraverbal communication is a two-way process, as service users will also use this tool to assess whether workers are interested in their situation or are going through the motions. In this respect we would like to stress the importance of workers keeping to appointments and the times set. Failure to do this gives an all-too-clear message to service users that they are not as valued or important as the worker, providing the basis for a relationship that has from the outset disempowered the service user.

Written communication is the last area we would like to consider. Whilst this tends to reflect the outcome of meetings between service users and workers, such communications are also important in terms of that relationship. Written communication is mainly required by employers and other agencies to reflect the worker's assessment of the service user's situation (Thompson 2002). As such it needs to be written in an appropriate style for that context. However, reports can also be part of a growing practice of sharing our conclusions with service users and checking out their understanding of what has occurred and what will occur. In addition, under the provisions of the Data Protection Act 1998, service users have a right of access to information that is kept on their files. Consequently, two key areas stand out in this activity: what we know (facts) and what we believe (opinions). Failure to draw out these distinctions on what are often permanent records can be confusing and labelling to those using the service (Thompson 2002), often leading to subsequent workers obtaining an opinion that is based on supposition rather than fact. Written records also need to be written with clarity and in a manner that makes them accessible to service users, avoiding jargon wherever possible. What becomes apparent in even the simplest of interactions with service users is that these are activities and processes where effective communication is of vital importance.

If communication is a skill that is well covered in social work texts, then the following areas of negotiation and decision-making have received less attention. In terms of negotiation this is in part because empowerment and partnership are relatively new concepts for workers, who are still working out how to apply them to practice. Historically most social work approaches would have been based on the worker or agency holding expertise and defining the solution if not the problem. This was not done alongside the service user, but done to them by either passive agreement or imposition. Partnership, on the other hand, implies that we are looking if not for agreement at least for some understanding or acceptance of what is to be achieved. This is a goal that requires all parties to be heard in relation to both the causes of the situation and possible solutions. By implication, partnership implies that all parties are able to make a contribution to this process. In essence it should be a process that empowers service users by valuing their unique contribution.

Negotiation, however, is an activity that is also based on what is possible, something that will be influenced by the statutory and agency context, the workers' skills and abilities, and the service users' willingness and ability to be part of the process. It is not about giving people what they want, but finding a solution acceptable to all parties with the intention of making change real and possible. In essence it implies that all parties are willing to compromise in order to achieve a workable consensus. This is a task that is more difficult for some social work approaches than others. In particular the individual pathology and procedural approaches, with their reliance on worker expertise, can be problematic. Workers holding these approaches will have to review their own power and acknowledge the expertise that the service user has to contribute to the process of assessment and intervention. Negotiation is a social work skill that is not just confined to the relationship between the service user and worker. It is also required if the worker or care manager is involved with other agencies or trying to obtain resources within his/her own organisation.

Negotiation from an empowering perspective is based on seeking out the commonalities rather than emphasising the differences between perspectives (Thompson 2000). All parties need to be open about their purpose and intentions and what they seek to achieve. It is also important that empowering practitioners seek to ensure that service users are provided with the support they may require in order to be genuine participants in the process. In order to be an effective partner in any negotiation, each side needs to have a clear understanding of their own situation, the areas where there is the potential for compromise and those areas that they regard as non-negotiable. Negotiation is part and parcel of any approach that claims to work in partnership with service users, as it brings them into the heart of the social work process by acknowledging and valuing what they can expect to receive and contribute to their situation.

Despite the move towards partnership and its attendant skill of negotiation, workers will still have to make decisions about who to involve, the relevance of information, courses of action to take, etc. Whilst these can and are shared across the agency and multidisciplinary setting, a key feature of social work is the activity of decision-making. It is an area that in child care and criminal justice has in recent years come under increasing scrutiny owing to the high-profile mistakes made by a small number of workers and agencies. However, whilst social work is characterised by high-profile and potentially contentious decisions, it is also an activity where workers on a daily basis make decisions that impact on service users and their lives. It is only recently, with the work of Terence O'Sullivan (1999), that this important area – decision-making – has been given increased attention. O'Sullivan stresses the need to counterbalance the increasing number of procedures and checklists which, whilst meant to enhance our decision-making, have increasingly bureaucratised the process. O'Sullivan (1999, p. XI) instead provides a framework to help us consider what should influence our decision-making activities. He sees this as a 'supporting structure of grouped ideas and concepts and ideas placed in relation to each other with the purpose of providing a map that social workers can use to order their minds and act with purpose and clarity in the situations they face'.

This framework is required because, in making decisions, workers are rarely working with information that provides certainty. In fact, they are often called upon to make decision quickly against a background of uncertainty, partial information, scarcity of resources and with service users who are using the service unwillingly. In this context there is no guarantee about the choices that are made and there is the potential for public retribution if the wrong decision is made. O'Sullivan, whilst not providing definitive answers, suggests a process that should enable more considered decision-making and, hopefully, effective outcomes. Whilst what will be an appropriate decision is open to debate, O'Sullivan (1999, p. 16) provides the following framework for making decisions. Decision makers should have:

● been critically aware of and taken into account the decision-making contexts;

● involved the client to the highest feasible level;

● been clear in their thinking and aware of their emotions;

● produced a well-reasoned frame of the decision situation that is consistent with the available information; and

● based their course of action on a systematic appraisal of the options.

Whilst O' Sullivan fully explains each of these concepts, it is worth elaborating on two of these so that the framework becomes clearer. In terms of context, we are taking into consideration factors such as the aim of intervention, agency and legal context as well as the service user's situation. Workers do not operate independently and any decision has to be considered with this in mind. The second issue is that decisions are not technical activities but can also be influenced by our thoughts and feelings about a situation. They will also be influenced by our past experience of similar situations, which will influence when we will act. In essence our experiences will influence the threshold/level at which we become concerned about a situation. Relating this to Tarjinder's behaviour in the above case scenario, the worker's past experience of similar situations might mean that he/she would act quickly on the issue of truancy as it could lead to failure to return to school. Alternatively, their experience might have been that once the parent (Sandeep) returned home, the situation returned to normal. Hence the worker's concern and threshold of action in relation to truancy would be much higher. This issue of different thresholds of concern for workers has been studied by Dalgleish (2000), who identified marked differences in decision-making amongst child and family social workers, despite having the same information. The worker's threshold of concern will also influence the decision that is made. There is a need, therefore, for our threshold to be openly reflected upon and examined in supervision for more consistent decisions to be made. Finally we would like to reiterate O'Sullivan's commitment to involving service users in the situation. Whilst we believe that this is good practice, it should also lead to more effective practice. However, there is no guarantee of this as workers with the most effective communication and negotiation skills, who have fully reflected on their choices, are still making a judgement; they are providing an assessment of the situation. What is important is that this should be done in an empowering manner that is open to challenge and evaluation by the service user, the agency and, in a growing number of circumstances, the wider public.

Summary of Chapter

1. Assessment is a process that requires workers constantly to evaluate new information against their understanding of the situation. It is about more than determining if a resource should be provided; it is also about developing an understanding and basis for present and future intervention.

2. The workers' approach has real and significant implications for the involvement of service users in the assessment process and what information is considered important. It influences whether partnership is about informing service users or about giving them a say over the decisions that impact on their lives and what model of assessment is applied in any given situation.

3. The process of assessment has increasingly been influenced by factors such as risk and partnership. This has shifted the focus of assessment from need to risk. What risk and partnership highlight is that assessment is a subjective activity that requires workers to be honest and open about the purpose and process of their assessment.

4. Whilst all social work intervention is based on assessment, ethical assessment is an activity based around a host of skills, including effective communication, sound negotiating skills and effective decision-making. Many of these skills may be at an early stage of development, which means that their application is often a problematic activity.

4

Methods of Intervention:
Purpose and Process

Methods of intervention provide theoretical underpinning and practical structure to the process of work over time with service users. They are as integral to the social work process as assessment, yet are less clearly documented in terms of the process of method selection. Arguably, in recent years methods have become less important for practitioners as social work agencies have given greater emphasis to assessment and immediate or short-term solutions (Howe 1996; Lymbery 2001). This is reinforced by the increasingly reactive nature of service provision and the perceived need for pragmatic solutions. In addition, the move towards care management has meant the use of particular methods has increasingly been located in specialist areas of service provision, thereby potentially reducing the necessity for workers to have knowledge of a range of methods. Workers' understanding of methods of intervention has therefore often become superficial, impacting adversely on their application in practice, with workers claiming to utilise a particular method when this is not evidenced in their practice (Thompson 2000). For example, workers often claim to be utilising a task-centred method when engaged in a programme of practical tasks or cite crisis intervention as the selected method based simply on the existence of serious anxiety or concern. In neither case is such a method of intervention actually adopted, despite being described by workers in those terms. Therefore, whilst methods of intervention should provide the basis for any ongoing intervention with service users, work undertaken often lacks structured planning and becomes reactive, responding to specific events or crises. Despite this shift towards a more reactive environment with its emphasis on assessment frameworks, workers still retain large workloads. Unless these are appropriately supported and supervised, individual workers are unlikely to feel in control of the work environment, potentially leading to stress and burn-out (Jones 2001; Charles and Butler 2004). Utilising methods of intervention provides the opportunity to structure and plan work and decide on priorities in response to service users' needs. Methods are rarely simple to utilise as they are underpinned by a range of skills on the part of the worker. How they are applied will also be strongly influenced by the approach of the worker.

When looking at the range of methods available, it is possible to conclude that most tend to follow a similar process of application: assessment, planning of goals, implementation, termination, evaluation and review. This process, however, tends to disguise their differences in practice. Some methods will go through this process in as little as three/four interactions between worker and service user; others may take much longer. The difference in time reflects how some methods place greater or lesser importance on factors such as personality or society, which will inform what type of intervention may be required to resolve these issues in the service user's situation. Milner and O'Byrne (1998) helpfully suggest that the different methods of intervention can be understood in terms of 'maps' that consider different perspectives on the same situation. Whilst a map will look at a particular area, the type of map used will determine the signposts and detail of information that is utilised. What is helpful about this map analogy is that it highlights that different types of information are legitimate, depending on the purpose of the intervention, and that the methods do not have to be in competition with each other and can in effect be complementary, depending on how detailed and comprehensive the work with service users needs to be.

Until the 1970s the main method used by workers was psychosocial casework, a long-term method that enabled consideration of how the service users' past influenced their present. The worker's role in this method was enabling the service user within a therapeutic relationship to resolve past issues to modify present behaviour. However, during the mid-to late 1970s this one-method approach to practice came under increasing challenge from a number of areas (Payne 1997). First, the growing radical social work movement was concerned that psychosocial casework created a practice that ignored structural issues, particularly the class dimension of many service users' situations. In so doing, it perpetuated a response that located the source of the problem and the solution in the individual rather than the unjust and unequal nature of society (Bailey and Brake 1975; Corrigan and Leonard 1978; Langan and Lee 1989). Secondly, in the new social service departments of the 1970s there was a concern that long-term methods alone were time-consuming and failed to meet the range of situations faced by the growing numbers of people using the service (Davies 1994). In addition, the emerging managerial environment meant that short-term methods, such as the task-centred, behavioural, group and community work methods, started to be viewed much more favourably. This shift opened the door to other methods and by the 1990s this had extended to include short-term solution-focused methods and care management (Milner 2001; Orme 2001). What this means for workers is that there are a number of methods of intervention available which potentially can facilitate a range of responses to meet the specific needs of those using the service, rather than service users being required to fit any one method favoured by worker or agency. The main methods available to workers at this point and examined in most social work texts (in alphabetical order rather than any notion of use or merit) are shown in Table 4.1.

This is by no means an exhaustive list, but gives a flavour of the range and types of methods that are potentially available to the individual social worker and agency.

Table 4.1 Methods of intervention

Method	*Focus for intervention*	*Main theorists in social work usages*
Behavioural work	Intervention targeting aspects of individual, observable behaviours. Draws on a range of theories of cognition	McGuire (2000); Sheldon (1995)
Brief-solution-focused work	A short-term, strengths-based method emphasising the utilisation of existing coping mechanisms/skills to resolve new challenges	De Shazer (1982); Milner (2001)
Care management *	'The process of identifying the social and health care needs of individuals in the community, together with the planning and delivery of integrated programmes designed to meet those needs.'	Orme and Glastonbury (1994); Coulshed and Orme (1998)
Community work *	'A wide-ranging set of practices designed to improve the quality of life for individuals within designated areas, geographical localities and communities.'	Popple (1995); Twelvetrees (2002)
Constructive social work	Based on a post-modern analysis, constructive social work explores the pluralities of human experience and the complex narratives we create to explain phenomena	Parton and O'Byrne (2000); Pease and Fook (1999)
Counselling *	'The process whereby a trained professional counsellor gives another person support and guidance in an individual or group setting.'	Brearley (1995); Seden (1999)

Continued

Table 4.1 Continued

Method	Focus for intervention	Main theorists in social work usages
Crisis intervention	A short-term method of intervention utilising a crisis situation as a catalyst for change	Thompson (1991); O'Hagan (1986)
Ecological/systems work *	'A perspective in social work that emphasises the adaptive and reciprocal relationship between people and their environment.'	Pincus and Minahan (1973); Bilson and Ross (1999)
Family work *	'A range of techniques and strategies for helping families to resolve relationship problems, attain goals and function more harmoniously.'	Walker (2004); Barnes (1998)
Feminist/narrative work *	'A diversity of social work approaches that have as their common element recognition of women's oppression and the aim of overcoming its effects.'	Dominelli (2002b); Langan and Day (1992); Hamner and Stratham (1999)
Group work *	'A range of activities, including a method of social work intervention, that can enable individuals and groups to develop problem-solving skills to address both their own concerns and those of members of the wider community.'	Brown (1992); Doel and Sawdon (1999); Douglas (1993)
Psychosocial	Based on psychodynamic theories that focus on the impact of past events on current lived experience – the interplay of psychological and societal influences.	Hollis (1972); Ryan (1993)
Structural social work	An analysis of social problems that locates them within the social and political structures rather than with the individual	Mullaly (1997)
Task-centred	A short-term systematic method focused on the contractual completion of achievable and agreed tasks	Doel (1992); Reid and Epstein (1972)

* Definitions taken from Pierson and Thomas (2002).

In most of the above methods it is the worker who provides the direct service, although with the development of care management this is no longer the sole way of working. Arguably, care management, which developed from the community care reforms of the early 1990s, has shifted the focus of social work practice also to include indirect service provision. This begs the question as to whether care management should be considered as part of the range of social work methods. If the definition of a method of intervention is a means of structuring work over time, then care management must have a legitimate claim for inclusion, albeit problematic in its execution. The role of the care manager is to plan and co-ordinate a package of care for the service user, using other workers either in the local authority or in the voluntary or private sector to deliver the component parts of this package (Orme and Glastonbury 1994; James 1994). At first glance, care management can appear similar to direct work carried out by the worker, requiring many of the same skills such as assessment, planning, co-ordination and evaluation (Coulshed and Orme 1998). However, this move towards indirect service delivery has led to concerns that the quality of provision to service users is being diluted by unqualified staff carrying out the direct work (Watson 2002). This occurs because the focus of care management differs from direct practice, creating a practice that, as Fook (2000, p.149) points out, will be:

- system- rather than service-user-focused;
- serve management rather than professional or service users' interests;
- be technocratic and simplistic rather than complex, holistic or long-term and, as a consequence, less responsive to personalised, individual needs;
- be driven by an economic, rationalist imperative.

In effect, she argues that, in the present environment, care management has lost its critical and empowering edge, giving more emphasis to service planning and resources than to service users' needs. Whilst resources are a crucial consideration for any worker providing a service, they are, arguably from a care management perspective, the starting point for intervention and all too often can shape the nature of service provision rather than the needs of the service user or any evaluation of risk. This emphasis on resources means that, in practice, care management often lends itself to assessment based on a procedural model, where the worker ensures that the right questions are answered to access the agency's provision (Smale et al. 1993). Whilst acknowledging the concerns that care management presents for the quality and professionalism of social work practice, it is our contention that this method can complement individual work rather than, as some fear, supersede it (Parton 1996) if it is utilised within an empowering framework.

What the growing range of methods of intervention has meant for individual workers is that there is less likelihood of them fitting the service user to their preferred or favourite method rather than fitting the method to the service user. Workers who restrict themselves to a method, or a limited range of methods, are likely to restrict the range of options they have for practice, thereby reducing their flexibility and potentially fitting the service user's needs to the worker's skills rather than the other way around.

The Process of Method Implementation

The fact that different methods have contradictory as well as complementary theoretical underpinnings poses a real challenge for workers. This is apparent through all stages of the process of method implementation. Each method, as we shall see in Chapters 5 and 6, has a different assessment and implementation process, which looks for different types of information about the service user's situation. For example, the task-centred method looks for information about causes and solutions in the service user's *present* situation; psychosocial casework, however, explores *past* experiences. Equally, the method of assessment employed may limit the worker's capacity to consider and utilise alternative methods of intervention. The issue for workers in relation to assessment is that, unless they develop a structure that enables them to keep as many of the methods as possible open to consideration, they will need to carry out at least two assessments: the first to obtain a general picture of the necessity for involvement; the second to negotiate the direct method of intervention with the service user. This is a potentially wasteful activity in terms of resources and one that does not fit with the managerial, cost-conscious environment. What is therefore required is an effective assessment framework that builds in flexibility and keeps options open in relation to the methods, but does not become too cumbersome or time-consuming in relation to the service user or worker. One means of doing this is to use a biography framework, which enables service users to locate their present issues within the context of their lives, both past and present (Dalrymple and Burke 1995). This framework for assessment requires the worker to consider the following areas early in the assessment process:

● What are the issues of concern for the service user and worker?

● What is their significance in terms of who the service user is? (past)

- What is their significance at this point of time? (present)

- What possible solution may deal with these problems?

What these questions should help to identify is the nature and source of the problems faced by service users. For example, if the situation and its antecedents are focused on past events, then this may suggest a psychosocial method; if they are more current, then short-term methods such as task-centred casework would obtain greater importance. If workers aspire to an empowering practice, the process of information-gathering should attempt to fit in with an exchange model of assessment, no matter what the subsequent method of intervention. This should also begin to provide the basis of a working relationship, moving towards partnership. This possibility of different responses can be seen in relation to John's situation.

John (84), as you will recall, had developed a pattern of contact with a range of public services that provided him with a sense of purpose and structure to his week. This pattern had not been clearly identified by the agencies concerned, and they tended to respond in a reactive manner to each individual point of referral. This type of response emerged because workers seemed to be focusing on his immediate needs as expressed by him, rather than assessing the pattern of issues that had been emerging over time. Many of John's requests for social work intervention, such as his debts and housing issues, related to issues that lent themselves to short-term methods of intervention. A psychosocial method, on the other hand, might have been an appropriate response to his feelings about losing his partner and coping with his changed status within his local community. Whilst it is important to adopt as holistic an assessment as possible, the pressing nature of many of his practical issues would suggest that these should be the immediate focus for intervention. What changed the nature of John's interactions with these agencies was the worker's view that John would not be able to begin to deal with his feelings of loss until he had been able to resolve at least some of the issues that were to him more immediate and urgent. Intervention, therefore, was focused on his identified needs, with a plan for future intervention around his issues of loss.

Separating out presenting and underlying issues early in the assessment process is crucial to providing an initial sense of focus for intervention but will need to be constantly reviewed with the service user. What it should provide is an opportunity for the worker to look at an assessment framework and strategy that facilitates long-term or short-term methods of intervention and consequently moves the assessment towards particular methods. The role of the worker's approach to practice is crucial. Empowering practice implies that workers move beyond narrow assessment frameworks linked to particular methods. This more inclusive and holistic assessment process should also enable the service user to have a direct influence on the method of intervention selected.

Each method's assessment process excludes possible solutions that could from a different perspective be important. Once a method of intervention has been assessed and agreed as appropriate to the service user's needs, its process will direct how it should be applied in practice over time (Compton and Galloway 1989; Evans and Kearney 1996). Our concern is that, throughout the literature on specific methods, the process of intervention is often described in a linear manner, giving the impression that this is a rational and sequential activity. In practice this is rarely the case, as the worker's ongoing relationship with the service user means that the methods and their implementation tend to be much more complex. First, the process of intervention (as with assessment) has to consider the issue of new and more detailed information as the relationship with the service user changes and develops. This is particularly marked in methods of intervention that are built around time-limited assessment tools. For example, in relation to behavioural work, it may be difficult for the worker to keep the task purely to the baseline issues drawn up at the time of assessment. This information can quickly become outdated and consequently require the worker and service user to review both the purpose and process of intervention. Secondly, many service users' lives can change relatively quickly and what was seen as a source of concern early in the process may no longer be so important or may have been overtaken by events (Bullock et al. 1998). Both these situations mean that whilst methods may appear to have a coherent logic, this is not always apparent in the service user's specific situation. That is not to say that workers should not have a clear plan which reflects their own and the service users' concerns, but that this may have to be adapted or changed to reflect changing circumstances.

This need to respond in a flexible manner remains equally true when we examine the final stages of any method: evaluation and termination. Review is an ongoing process throughout the period of the work, but specific evaluation should be built into the termination phase of the method (Payne 1997). In doing this, both the worker and service user will assess and reassess whether the method is working and if they are succeeding in the task that has been set. It should also help to return to the baseline purpose for intervention, thereby determining whether to re-evaluate the method's applicability or continue on the chosen path of action. For example, when considering the notion of termination, there are a number of factors that are directly linked to the work with the service user.

These are:

- Has the threshold of concern now been sufficiently diminished to suggest that intervention is no longer required?

- Does the method of intervention need to change? If not, is the work to continue, in what way and with whom?

- Does the previous involvement suggest that the situation continues to merit the priority given?

Factors that influence any decision to terminate involvement include the wider demands of the agency, the worker's ability to manage workloads, and the needs of the service user. Whilst these factors tend to be self-evident, they are often not taken into consideration by many workers, who struggle to close cases. The reasons for this tend to be varied, reflecting concerns about what is a legitimate threshold that would suggest that a 'good enough' service has been provided (Dalgleish 2000). The importance of a sound assessment process that is related to specific outcomes cannot be overstated. If workers do not have a clear understanding of the aims of their intervention, how can they know when it has been concluded? When a baseline for the work is not set, this may mean that even when the agreed tasks have been completed the worker and service user find reasons to continue involvement. Such work may be important but, if it is to be undertaken, it requires further assessment and prioritisation. Where this does not happen, there is a danger of drifting into new pieces of work that may lead to a growing dependency on the part of both the service user and worker (Seligman 1992).

The Influence of the Worker's Approach on Method Selection

So far we may have given the impression that using methods is about dipping into the social worker's tool-kit (Trevithick 2000) to see what best matches the situation. This tool-kit analogy, whilst helpful, has its limitations in practice. The worker's approach can and will influence the tools that they consider are appropriate for the task. Some methods, within a particular approach, may not be considered ethical or the workers' skills may not be sufficient to carry out the form of intervention required. In our experience the two methods that most often fall into this category are the behavioural and psychosocial methods. In relation to the former, a concern is that this, in its traditional form, can be considered unethical as the worker is perceived as having the potential to manipulate the situation without the service user's knowledge or consent. With regard to the psychosocial method, it is the underpinning theory that is perceived as complex, thereby influencing the implementation of the method. In relation to methods being used unethically, the workers' approach will affect how they perceive and adapt them to specific situations. The implementation of methods, therefore, is affected both by the intrinsic values of the method and by the value base of the individual worker.

Whilst it would be nice to think that each of the approaches would be able to incorporate and adapt all the methods, this is arguably not feasible. The underlying premise of some methods can be incompatible with or contradict the theory that the approach is based upon. Methods are not neutral tools that any worker can draw upon but a way of working that reflects not just different situations but explanations for those situations. Consequently, they either fit a particular approach or tend to challenge its underpinning assumptions. Whilst trying not to be too prescriptive, it is possible to envisage the three approaches resonating with the methods shown in Table 4.2. Even when a method is compatible and consistent with an approach, the worker will influence how it is applied in practice, shaping the method's implementation and evaluation. This can be seen in relation to the task-centred method, which has a congruence with both the procedural and progressive approaches. For example, at its most simple, a task-centred assessment (see Chapter 5) within the procedural approach is likely to involve the worker determining what information is important and then influencing the definition of the problem. Within a progressive approach, assessment would be carried out alongside the service user, who should through negotiation agree both the issues to address and how this would be done. This simple example highlights how the workers' perception of their expertise and consequently their approach shapes the method, in particular their attitude to what empowerment and partnership mean for practice. No method is a purely technical activity, therefore, but reflects the values and understanding of the workers using

Table 4.2 Possible linkage of methods to approaches

Procedural	Behavioural work, care management, crisis intervention, ecological/systems work, group work and task-centred
Individual pathology	Crisis intervention, family work, group work, psychosocial counseling
Progressive	Brief-solution-focused work, community work, constructive work, task-centred work, feminist/narrative work, group work and structural social work

it in practice. For example, the task-centred method is often perceived as empowering with black service users and other oppressed groups (Ahmad 1990). This occurs because service users are able to define their own problems. However, it ignores the fact that a practitioner using an approach which is agency- or worker-focused may not fully enable the service user to define the problem. Instead they may inform the service users but not engage them in the process of determining priorities or how these should be achieved. Hence the process of involvement would mean the service user being empowered at the level of customer rather than citizen (Clarke and Newman 1997). When we consider this method from an emancipatory perspective, citizenship would imply a method where service users are involved in defining priorities, possible solutions and action. In this respect, empowerment becomes a real and everyday issue in the worker's practice and the service user's experience. Empowerment is not just about the grand strategies of life, it is also important in the day-to-day actions of the people with whom we are working, enabling them to face the challenges of their lives and situations. Empowerment and partnership in this context would, for example, include sharing and involving the service user in areas such as:

- method selection
- the specific application of method in context
- the allocation of tasks/responsibilities within the work
- the process of evaluation and review.

This presents a real challenge for workers, who would clearly be opening their practice to scrutiny by service users. It may not be as simple or straightforward as imagined. Many service users are not used to being involved in this level of information-sharing and may not want or be ready for this form of practice. At a point of personal crisis, service users may be happy to accept a rather didactic approach from workers. It may be easier to accept what is offered rather than find the emotional energy required to negotiate something different. Service users may need to acquire new skills in order to be able to take full advantage of the partnership being offered. Young people, for example, need to be helped to utilise their legal right to participate in decisions made about their future care (Thomas and O'Kane 1999). Both the worker and the service user therefore need time to develop their knowledge and skills if empowerment is to become a practice reality. This needs to link to the workers' approach to practice and will evolve over time as they become more skilled and confident in their chosen approach.

The interdependence of method and approach can be illustrated through John's situation. Utilising a task-centred method with John and taking a procedural approach, the *worker* would be likely to assess and define the areas for work, leading to potential solutions being identified by him/her within current agency resources. This is not dissimilar to the agency's original response to John. Each time he called at the agency, he was met with a response to the presenting problem as defined by the worker. This appeared not to meet John's needs.

By adopting a task-centred method and taking a progressive approach, *John* would be likely to be encouraged to provide what he considered to be the important information about his situation and to identify what assistance he required. He would be viewed as being the expert in his own life, with the capacity to define his needs in his own terms. Using this approach, the worker would assist John to identify potential solutions based on his own resources as well as those of the agency (e.g. his wider social networks).

While it may be tempting for workers to work within their own 'comfort zone', approaches to practice are important indicators of outcome in terms of the way that the service is experienced by service users.

Using Methods: Personal Organisation and Workload Management

As we have seen, using methods of intervention can be a complex activity that is demanding of workers at a number of levels, none more so than that of their time and energy. In the present social work environment this is rarely acknowledged, as it is assumed that the growing use of short-term methods is less intensive and demanding of the worker as well as more successful in practice. This, in our opinion, is a misconception, as the more popular short-term methods often make extensive demands on the workers' time and energy. They should not, therefore, be utilised unless the worker is able to provide the resources required properly to carry out the intervention. Just how demanding methods of intervention can be in practice can be seen from the following simple example. Working with a service user using a method of intervention on a weekly basis may take up at least two to four hours of the worker's week, taking into account direct contact, case records, carrying out of worker's task, etc. Therefore, by definition, this limits the number of service users that any social worker is effectively able to work with in a planned way at any given point in time.

Consequently, to use methods of intervention means that workers have to be well organised at a personal level to ensure that they are able proactively to carry out the task. This reality challenges much of the reactive culture that has grown around social work practice over the last 30 years and has led to a growing concern for social work agencies to adopt workload or caseload management systems (Orme 1995; Thompson 2000).

Workload management should be an activity that looks at the full range of tasks undertaken by the individual worker and is concerned with matching what they can provide to the demands on their time and the needs of the agency. While far from being an exact science, it does at least provide a crude indication of the allocation of time and resources against which workers can begin to measure their effectiveness (Orme 1995). This can enable workers to obtain control over their workload, by quantifying and prioritising what they do over a period of work time. This is required not just to enable individual workers to prioritise methods, but also to enable social service agencies to find a way of filtering out what work needs to be and can be carried out in the face of increasing demand for the service. Caseload management, on the other hand, is more specific in that it attempts to look at what priority workers are giving to their 'cases' and involves a review of this activity against worker and agency objectives (Vickery 1977; Orme and Glastonbury 1994). Workers require some system of caseload management to enable them to start to make sense of the many and competing demands made by service users and to prioritise those that lend themselves to the systematic application of methods. If such priorities are not set, this can lead to large caseloads that create stress and anxiety for the worker. Caseload management also provides a framework for negotiating and limiting such demands in order that workers can realistically and effectively provide a professional service. As we shall explore in Chapter 8, this takes place within a supervisory relationship which workers must learn to manage effectively to secure their desired outcomes. We do not intend here to highlight any particular caseload management system but, instead, consider some of the principles that should underpin any system that is adopted to help workers make sense of their situation. However, we would strongly advocate that some system be used as this avoids the all-too-frequent practice of drift in relation to the work. This is a situation where workers may adopt quick-fix, routinised responses rather than structured interventions over time, often disempowering service users and rarely effecting real change in their lives. The key to most caseload management systems is that they provide a structured and transparent means of allocating scarce resources to respond fairly to the needs of service users. This process implies a rational and logical approach. It moves beyond what Vickery (1977) claims is a common response where priority is given to those who are most vociferous, those perceived as being the responsibility of the social work domain and those with whom workers have a personal empathy. Whilst Vickery was writing about this issue almost thirty years ago, it still has strong echoes in modern practice, reflecting a culture which responds automatically to certain demands of the agency or service users and can easily lead to a downward spiral of reactive and unplanned work. This can for many service users mean that they have little chance of receiving a reliable service which respects the commitments that have been made to keep to agreed work times. It would be easy to 'blame the worker' here and to attribute the failings of service delivery to that individual. That, in our view, would be to misunderstand completely the nature of the problem. Professional workers are often attempting to prioritise their involvement with service users against a context, both local and national, of almost constant change. It is not possible for individual workers, for example, to decide on the agreed priorities of the agency, particularly in the current environment of integrated service delivery. Social work ethics and values demand that workers attempt to provide an appropriate level of service within the managerial constraints that may apply. This is not easy and may be the source of much of the day-to-day stress on individual workers (Jones 2001; Lymbery and Butler 2004). Key to this process is assessment, which should enable workers to prioritise work on the basis of need and risk, thereby enabling them to make the following decisions in relation to work that they see as ongoing, rather than that which will be caseload-managed or not given a service:

- Does this situation require urgent attention?

- If it is urgent, will it be appropriately dealt with by immediate practical support or does it require structured intervention using methods?

- Can I safely leave this structured work until later, given minimal support, supervision and monitoring?

- How does the situation fit with the priorities set by the agency?

The answer to these questions should enable the worker to begin to prioritise and structure their workload around low- and high-priority situations faced by service users and agency. Whilst this activity is crucial to enable workers to keep control of their time, this 'pruning' activity needs to be done within the supervisory relationship in order for the agency to be part of the process and to be aware of what is considered important in the worker's caseload. Both workers and managers will then be aware of why some cases are worked with more frequently than others. However, in undertaking this activity, it is crucial that workers keep to a minimum the amount of work that is considered urgent and needing structured intervention. As we have already seen, structured methods of intervention are very demanding of time and energy. Given the extensive demands on workers' time and energy, realistically they could only work with four or five service users using methods at any given point of time. Given the example above, a minimum of about four hours per week, four structured interventions would entail 16–20 hours' work being undertaken in any working week. This is a very high percentage of any worker's time, given that there will be other service users to consider and monitor, plus reports, supervision, etc.

What this prioritisation means in practice is that service users who do not fit the priority for being worked with using methods will need to be monitored and enabled to wait until it is possible to provide an appropriate service. While it is difficult to 'ration' workers' time in this way, it is essential if the overall quality of service provision is not to be diluted. If not addressed, workers risk moving back into a vicious circle where the work is never completed and the response to service users is reactive and crisis-driven. Monitoring situations until they can be fully worked with involves more than just visiting to see if 'things are still all right'. It needs regular reassessment and re-evaluation of the changing circumstances of the service user. It also needs workers to look at practical, time-limited ways of alleviating or changing the situation, which do not detract from the time required for other prioritised service users. Having responded to Susan's immediate practical needs, for example, it may be that the worker will negotiate an appropriate starting point for the more structured psychosocial intervention required. Caseload management requires workers constantly to balance priorities and be realistic about what they can possibly achieve in any given situation. They will be working, therefore, with service users whom they see frequently and with whom they have adopted formal methods of intervention and others whom they see regularly, but on a much less frequent basis, i.e. monitoring the situation. Both types of intervention should be clearly structured and have a purpose, but that will vary given the priority allocated to each service user's situation. The danger with this model is the tendency for those not prioritised to drift. Workers need to use their less frequent monitoring visits to ensure that both they and the service user are clear about the purpose of the service at that point in time. A handy survival technique which we have found useful in terms of operating this type of system is where workers, as far as possible, concentrate their high-priority and low-priority work into specific days of the week. This 'chunking' of time should enable workers to start to structure their week into distinct activities and is also a visible reminder of the priority and purpose given to the different types of work.

With changing work patterns and the sharing of responsibilities, however, this may not be possible. In terms of the social work process, therefore, it is our contention that planned methods of intervention will be necessary to provide a basis for action over time. This can only be achieved, in our view, by a systematic and structured approach to workload. While managers may claim the 'right to manage', professionally qualified social workers must also take responsibility for the constraints inherent in their own planned approach to practice. Workers need to have some system of caseload management in order to be able to utilise planned intervention over time, i.e. methods.

Empowering Service Users in the Utilisation of Methods

Given that methods and their implementation can be a complex activity, it is important that, as far as possible, what is being undertaken and by whom is clear to all parties. It requires workers formally to conceptualise and explain their actions. There have been increasing moves towards developing verbal or written agreements that acknowledge all the participants' roles and responsibilities. Using such agreements can help avoid clashes in perspective that often occur because of hidden assumptions or issues not being dealt with in agreed priority (Lishman 1994). Such factors, if not dealt with, can lead to the breakdown of trust and may influence any subsequent work between service user and worker. Written agreements have gained importance, as they are seen as encouraging honesty where the purpose of intervention and responsibility for the work have been shared openly by the service user and the worker. To be able to undertake this task, workers need to be able to negotiate with service users around what is to be achieved and by whom, including their own and agencies' inputs. However, we would like to caution about making these written agreements and subsequent tasks or goals too vague and consequently difficult to achieve, particularly for the service user. For example, in relation to Susan there is no point agreeing that she should provide better parenting, as this is at best vague, at worst meaningless. What would be more appropriate is to look at how she could set limits around bedtimes for the children and what she could do to make this a reality. This would be a tangible and achievable task that could be supported by the worker, enabling Susan to feel she was being supported to reach her goals. When used in this manner, written agreements provide the potential for an empowering practice that involves partnership with those using the service. However, what written agreements do not provide is a guarantee of improved practice. If they are no more than a set of tasks that the service user has to carry out, with no prior negotiation and no reciprocal commitment and obligations by the worker, then they will not encourage change or address the issue of empowerment and oppression. Written agreements, depending on how they are used, have the potential not only to be open and empowering but also to hold service users to account for activities and goals that they have no possibility of achieving. In effect, they can be used to set the service user up for almost inevitable failure. Therefore, unless written agreements are based on negotiation, openness and honesty, they will not challenge the power differential between service user and worker and in effect can be used to reinforce or strengthen that difference (Rojek and Collins 1988).

Whilst we have used the term 'written agreements', it would be fair to say there is some concern about this terminology, particularly when workers talk about them as contracts (Corden and Preston-Shoot 1987). The term 'contract' has connotations of being legal and formally binding, which some contracts are. This is rarely the case in the social work context. Therefore, it may be more appropriate to think of them as 'agreements', as this suggests working together in partnership, looking for people to invest in rather than be bound by the process of intervention. In addition, verbal agreements are limited in their potential by the fact that they are based on word of mouth. This makes them open to differences in memory recall and also may advantage those with better verbal/language-processing skills. Consequently, in our opinion, agreements should be in writing whenever practicable as they provide service users with the opportunity to reflect on what they are agreeing to and check that their recollections are accurate. When workers are negotiating and making agreements with service users, these are not set in tablets of stone. It is particularly important that service users have the opportunity to influence the agreement and to make any changes that they consider necessary as the work progresses. This may mean that they need to be given the opportunity to seek independent advice, either from within their own social networks or from other professionals, including solicitors. While this may place workers in a difficult position in terms of their agency perspective, the opportunity to hold workers to account for their practice is very important. Accountability is an important aspect of the professional role and is, in a number of areas, reinforced by statute (Preston-Shoot 2001). If workers enter into formal agreements with service users, the desired outcomes need to be clear on both sides – as do the potential consequences that may be applied. An empowering approach to practice implies a willingness to engage with the process of accountability in a professional manner. To take advantage of complaints procedures, for example, may require services users to seek advice from external sources.

Recent years have seen a growth in formats provided by agencies for written agreements with service users, for example in criminal justice. These written agreements vary considerably in their complexity and formality and some have the potential to provide confusion as well as clarity. However, it is our belief that written agreements should be kept as clear and straightforward as possible in order that they can be understood and used by both worker and service user. There is a real danger that they will become paper exercises rather than working documents providing clarity and purpose to intervention and practice. Therefore, with this goal in mind, we offer an illustrative example:

Written Agreement between Anywhere Council and Mr John Brown

Introduction

This agreement has been drawn up jointly in response to Mr Brown's request for assistance with his current financial difficulties and his desire to be rehoused. The agreement takes account of the fact that, at 84 years old, Mr Brown's ability to undertake practical tasks is limited. Mr Brown wishes to be rehoused in smaller accommodation that will be easier to maintain and is closer to amenities. He is currently unable to be considered for transfer owing to his rent arrears and outstanding bills for gas and electricity. The purpose of intervention at this time is to offer time-limited, targeted support to help Mr Brown resolve these difficulties. The agreed method of intervention will be task-centred casework over eight sessions that will take place in Mr Brown's home on Wednesdays at 11 a.m. for a maximum of one hour.

Agency Responsibilities

Ann Smith, Care Manager, will contact the housing agency and gas and electricity suppliers to obtain an accurate account of the monies outstanding.

A full welfare benefits check will be conducted by the welfare rights office and the outcome posted to Mr Brown at his home address.

Ann Smith will, with Mr Brown's co-operation, produce a proposed schedule of repayments to meet the requirements of the agencies involved. This will take full account of Mr Brown's ability to meet such repayments while maintaining a reasonable lifestyle.

Ann Smith will discuss potential areas of housing stock that may be suitable to meet Mr Brown's needs and will arrange for him to visit and make his own assessment of suitability.

Ann Smith will attempt to attend each planned session. In the event that this is not possible, she will contact Mr Brown to discuss possible alternatives. Cancellation will only occur in exceptional circumstances.

Mr Brown's Responsibilities

Mr Brown will provide all the documentation necessary to explore his financial situation, including account numbers, contact persons, etc.

Mr Brown will meet with the welfare rights officer within the next two weeks to explore his existing benefits and will complete any paperwork necessary to apply for any additional allowances to which he may be entitled.

Mr Brown will meet with Ann Smith at his home each Wednesday at the time agreed above. He will advise Ann, if possible in advance, if he cannot keep any of these appointments.

Practical Issues to be Considered

Given Mr Brown's financial circumstances, all letters and telephone calls will be made from Ann's office.

Transport will be arranged to take Mr Brown to view alternative housing stock.

An application will be made by Ann on Mr Brown's behalf to secure funding for the installation of a telephone for him.

Monitoring and Review of this Agreement

Each time they meet, Ann and Mr Brown will evaluate the progress made and make any adjustments required to keep the agreement on track.

Both parties will be able to discuss any issues that have arisen which interfere with their ability to complete their allotted tasks. Wherever possible, timescales will be adjusted to take account of any such new information.

Desired Outcomes

Mr Brown considers a successful outcome to be the full resolution of his financial difficulties and the securing of a new tenancy.

Ann views this as an ambitious aim but considers sufficient easing of the financial difficulties to negotiate with the housing agency for a transfer to be a good measure of success. Securing Mr Brown's full benefit entitlement will be a good basis upon which to build his future financial security.

Clearly there are many situations where the process of creating an agreement in written form will be affected by the ability of the service user to be fully involved in such a process. By adopting a flexible and creative approach to the task, the process can be genuinely inclusive, regardless of the limitations imposed by the needs of the service user. Therefore, whilst written agreements are not the panacea for all social work's ills, they do provide the potential to address one of the key concerns raised by service users – that workers are often vague, lack purpose and are uncertain about their role and purpose (Howe 1987). As we have identified at the beginning of this chapter, methods of intervention provide a means of structuring and planning work over time. Written agreements should provide the worker and the service user with a basis for working in partnership where both the means and ends have been negotiated and agreed and all parties know what is expected of them.

Summary of Chapter

1. Methods of intervention provide a rationale to the structuring of work over time. The stages of intervention of most methods are assessment, action, evaluation and termination. There is a real need for workers to give increased importance to utilsing methods in order to move their caseloads beyond a mainly reactive response to practice.

2. How methods are applied and utilised in relation to service users will reflect the values and practice embodied in the worker's approach and the exigencies of the service user's situation. In other words, they will either be empowering or not, dependent on how they are utilised by the worker and to what effect.

3. Using structured methods of intervention with service users is undoubtedly a time-consuming activity. Whilst there are numerous models of caseload management that workers can utilise, what is important is that they should be adopted and used within the supervisory relationship. This accountability process protects not only the service user but also the worker.

4. Methods of intervention are often complex and difficult to explain simply and clearly to service users. If they are to be used in an empowering manner it is important that all parties should be clear, as far as possible about what is being undertaken and by whom. Formal agreement can be helpful, enabling all parties to reflect on what has been agreed and achieved. However, it is crucial that these should be developed in an open manner, negotiated with the service user and reflect not just the worker's but also the service user's concerns.

5

Methods of Intervention: Working with Presenting Issues

For most social work practitioners, developing a portfolio of methods tends to be a rather pragmatic activity influenced by professional training, the exigencies of the agency and the individual worker's approach to practice. While developing a range of methods may be a complex activity within the current practice context, it does provide workers with a structured rationale for intervention. We have chosen to consider the purpose and process of a small number of methods in order that readers may select those which they consider relevant to their situation. Our intention is to introduce the reader to each of the selected methods, providing as we go some useful reference points for further study. Our primary aim is to encourage readers to explore these methods by arguing that it is the approach of the worker that impacts significantly on the process of intervention and its potential outcomes for the service user. The choice of methods for any text has to be fairly arbitrary. The methods in this and the following chapter have been selected because we consider them to be those most commonly used in social work settings. We accept that this is an assumption on our part, as there has been little research on the relative utilisation of different methods. However, our experience as practitioners and academics would suggest that the task-centred, behavioural work, psychosocial and crisis intervention methods are those which most workers would claim to use. We could have looked at the group work method (Douglas 1993; Doel and Sawdon 1999) or the increasingly popular solution-focused methods (De Shazer 1982; Parton and O'Byrne 2000). Both are relevant in many social work settings and are undoubtedly part of the professional social work agenda. Solution-focused methods in particular would appear potentially to bridge the gap between the managerial agenda and professional practice, providing intervention that is cost-effective and empowering for the service user. It also challenges the 'looking for problems' perspective of many other methods. Instead, its future-orientated, cognitive perspective develops positive solutions by placing service users as the experts in their own lives. The worker's role then becomes one of enabling service users to find alternatives to their present situation, using techniques such as the 'miracle question' or 'scaling' (Milner 2001). In using these techniques, it is intended that service users will be able to obtain a more positive picture of their strengths and build upon these in their future actions. This method is undoubtedly gaining currency in both the work environment and academic literature. Whilst we accept that there is a danger that our selection may reinforce the use of particular methods, our focus is on enabling workers to build on their present knowledge and skills in order for the methods to be utilised in a positive and empowering manner with the service user.

The methods chosen are presented in a structured manner, which includes underpinning theory, assessment, implementation, termination/ evaluation and concerns. This can give the impression that all methods follow the same logical structure, which is not true. As we have already seen, methods reflect the world of uncertainty that is characteristic of social work. Any structure is at best a framework for our understanding that will in reality be unlikely to follow such a logical process. Therefore, whilst formalised structures help provide a clarity to our understanding, they also tend to simplify and underplay the subtleties of the process of intervention with specific service users. However, we have chosen this framework because it provides a starting point for understanding the application of the methods and the opportunity to look at the similarities and differences between them. What we have not considered in depth is the different emphasis in skills that goes with each of the methods. Different methods require different skills-mixes for the practitioner to make them effective, for example, the task-centred method requires workers to be organised and structured in their work in order for them to be able to give time to this highly demanding method. The psychosocial method, on the other hand, whilst requiring workers to be organised, also requires 'emotional intelligence' and communication skills, as this is more of a talking solution to service user problems.

Finally, the outline of the methods is not meant to be seen as definitive but to provide a starting point that you may wish to use as the basis for further exploration and understanding. We have tried to locate the methods within the empowerment debate and explore how likely they are to fit the individual or democratic agenda. To take this forward, workers need to develop their understanding. We would urge you to read the original texts as well as more current sources in each of the methods and then seek appropriate support and training to learn how to put these into practice. Good practitioners, therefore, have to work at developing their professionalism, constantly looking to increase their understanding of themselves and their insight and skills. This chapter is the start, not the end, of that process.

The two methods that will be considered in this chapter are the task-centred and the behavioural method. They have been selected because both deal with presenting issues and are based on the service user developing problem-solving skills to change his/her situation. Arguably, in the present managerial climate of what works and can be measured, both these methods with their underpinning short-term philosophy and clear, measurable goals/outcomes are finding favour. Both appear popular with workers, although the behavioural method, despite its evidenced success in a number of areas (Sheldon and Chilvers 2000), still seems to be resisted by many practitioners because of ethical concerns. This will be discussed again later in the chapter.

Task-centred casework

The task-centred method is a time-limited method which focuses on the service user and worker jointly resolving surface issues and concerns. Unlike other methods of intervention, this has not been borrowed from other disciplines, but has originated within and been created specifically for social work. It has been based on developing the experience of practitioners and researchers in both North America (Reid and Epstein 1972, 1977) and the United Kingdom (Goldberg et al. 1977, 1985) who were concerned to provide problem-focused intervention that could demonstrate its effectiveness. These original texts by Reid and Epstein still have validity for understanding the method and, in our opinion, continue to provide an excellent starting point for understanding task-centred work. Underpinning this method is the claim that it is applicable to most social work settings and has been used with many different groups and individuals, including those of diverse cultural backgrounds (Doel and Marsh 1992). In particular, Reid (1978) claims that the method is effective in dealing with the following wide range of issues faced by service users:

- interpersonal conflict

- dissatisfaction in social relationships

- problems with formal organisations

- difficulty in role performance

- decision problems

- reactive emotional stress

- inadequate resources

- psychological and behavioural problems.

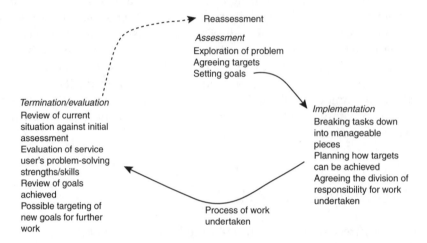

Figure 5.1 Task-centred casework

Underpinning theory

Much has been made of the fact that this method does not have a distinct theory base. Whilst there is no explicit theory underpinning this method, it is based on the assumption that surface/presenting problems are important and need to be worked on to enable change. This means that certain responses obtain less prominence, such as those which suggest that issues may be beneath the surface, related to past experiences. Therefore, despite the method's claim to be theory-free, it is based on assumptions about how people function, change and develop within society (Milner and O'Byrne 2002).

In the more empowering application of the method is the belief that the service users' perceptions of the problem are what counts, as they are seen as the experts on their own situation. It is this acknowledgement of the centrality of the service user which has resulted in the task-centred method being seen as having the potential to promote partnership between the worker and the service user (Marsh 1997; Coulshed and Orme 1998). It does this by enabling service users to explain the context of their situations and to develop the means to achieve change. In this respect, the method places the presenting issues of the service users as the problem and not the service users themselves. This may be why it has been welcomed by diverse racial groups as a method of working. Coulshed and Orme (1998, p. 123) describe the method, as 'an antidote to the process of labelling which assumes that being black is a problem'.

Task-centred work is time-limited and should involve a maximum of twelve regular interviews/sessions within three months, based on the theory that clear goals which are time-limited will motivate and create change (Reid and Epstein 1977). It is also premised on the belief that small changes which are achieved are more important than grand failures, as it will only compound the service users' difficulties if they do not achieve success (Doel and Marsh 1992). Consequently, a key to effective work is limited and achievable goals agreed in an open manner between the service user and the worker, each of whom will be expected to share his or her views and beliefs about the given situation. In doing this, it is argued that dependency is reduced as service users are empowered to make their own assessment of what can or cannot be achieved. This openness is reflected throughout the process of the method, enabling exploration of progress and any redefining of goals that may be required. Finally, the task-centred method is a *doing* method which involves all parties working on what has to be changed. What it is not about, however, is solely the completion of practical tasks (Marsh 1994). The *doing* in this method is part of a negotiated and well-planned piece of work that has a purpose and overall goal. It is based on an assessment of the issues to be addressed and the goals agreed with the service user, which are usually formally acknowledged by an agreement either written or formulated in a manner which best meets the needs of the service user (Doel 2002).

Assessment, implementation and termination/evaluation (see Figure 5.1)

Assessment

Assessment in task-centred work is, according to Doel (2002), based around three specific stages: exploring the problems, agreeing the targets and setting the goals. The focus of this assessment is not to study service users' emotional responses or past experiences, but to identify the issues of current concern in the service users' world and what are the obstacles to change. In this context, assessment means exploring and prioritising the service users' presenting problems. Assessment, like the method, is time-limited and should not extend beyond the first two to four sessions between the worker and service user. The focus of these initial sessions is to develop an overview of the situation and then prioritise the identified problems. Once the breadth of issues has been identified, the next stage is setting them in order of priority as a focus for future work. It is important to choose no more than two or three specific problems to work on, as this keeps the method manageable for both service user and worker. The problems selected are then looked at in more detail, with the intention of setting clear, modest and achievable goals for change. The role of the worker at this stage should be to establish what the service user really wants/needs to change (Milner and O'Byrne 1998). In terms of the method's success, it is important that as far as possible the priorities should be those of the service users, as arguably this encourages greater investment in the change process. However, negotiating goals that are feasible and desirable can often prove problematic owing to the statutory basis of intervention (Marsh 1997). What this can mean in practice is that legal constraints, together with any other potential obstacles, may have to be explained or clarified between the worker and service users.

Once the goals have been agreed, the next stage is to discuss how they can be achieved. Each goal is broken down into smaller tasks, which Doel and Marsh (1992, p. 62) describe as 'discrete parts of the overall action, a series of incremental steps towards goals'. In this respect, tasks are the stepping-stones towards the overall goal. If service users specify an unrealistic task, the worker will need to take time with them to identify how this may have to be modified to fit the larger goal. Implicit in clarifying tasks is negotiation and agreement about the role of the worker and the service user and about who does what, when and why. The worker's role at this stage may also involve negotiating with other agencies or carrying out immediate tasks to clear the way for the service user to become involved (Marsh 1997). In relation to Susan, this meant the worker negotiating with both her own agency and with nursery services in order to obtain safety equipment for the home and some personal time for Susan away from her children. This work was carried out to create the space for her and the worker to use task-centred practice to work on other issues such as finances and housing. However, whilst both parties are involved in the work, emphasis should be on the service user performing most of the tasks, either alone or with the worker's assistance. This is encouraged in order to enable service users to gain confidence in their own abilities and to discourage dependency on the 'expert' and 'capable' worker. During the assessment process a written contract should be agreed that is used to express what targets have been set, including time limits, and what work is to be undertaken to achieve the desired outcomes. It should also specify aspects such as the frequency of meetings, the venue, agreed record-keeping, the date for final review and the mechanism for renegotiating goals if required (Doel 2002).

Process of Implementation

Once an agreement has been formalised, task implementation is the next stage, and the focus of subsequent work. During this stage, the worker and the service user begin to break down the overall task into manageable chunks of activity. Such tasks may not necessarily be the most pressing but they are likely to be selected because their successful completion provides a confidence which enables the service user to move on to perhaps more complex tasks (Marsh 1994). This requires planning and thinking about how the tasks can be achieved. In practice, workers and service users may not always identify the most pressing situations to work on, but those that they feel have the greatest chance of success. This is where a clearly designed inclusive assessment becomes very important. In working in this reflective way, it is intended that service users (and workers) can see how obstacles to problem-solving can be overcome and can learn new strategies for solving further and future problems. Once these tasks have been agreed, the key skill for the worker in relation to service users is to support and enable them to take as much responsibility as they are capable of accepting for the task and to support them throughout the intervention process.

Ongoing evaluation of the situation, particularly by the worker, is crucial to ensure that the service user and worker are on the right track. In task-centred work, the assessment stage is relatively short, which means that more information will come to light as the worker/service user relationship develops. As new issues arise, workers, in collaboration with the service user, must decide in terms of their ongoing assessment whether it is appropriate or necessary to reformulate the tasks and goals. That reassessment may confirm and add to the tasks and goals that have already been agreed. The worker may, however, be faced with reviewing the planned tasks against a background of constantly changing information. This has the potential to throw the identified goals into disarray. Workers and service users are more inclined, therefore, to stick to the initial goals that have been agreed unless these are fundamentally undermined by new information. Ongoing assessment should, however, benefit both worker and service user as it enables them to see what they have accomplished and to assess the success of the set tasks. It also provides the worker with the opportunity to give service users recognition for what they have achieved, thereby enhancing their sense of empowerment and self-worth.

Planning is a crucial aspect of task-centred practice. It not only involves identifying tasks to be worked on but also requires clarity about how they will be carried out and by whom. Sessions at this stage will therefore include detailed discussion of how the task will be undertaken, who will do what and what is needed for this to be accomplished. This will involve the worker and the service user identifying strengths and limitations in relation to the tasks, working on these areas, and using techniques such as role play and rehearsal (Ford and Postle 2000). Returning to Susan, the initial sessions at this stage focused on her role-playing what she would say and why to the housing officials, in order to win their support for her relocation. This was based on both the worker and Susan breaking down the process to specific areas that she would have to cover at the interview with the housing authorities, thus enabling her to put this into practice with the housing agency. What should be aimed for, at this stage, is creating the basis for both the worker and the service user to carry out their tasks between the sessions. Work should be guided by, but not dependent on, the formal sessions for its completion. However, what this work with Susan also illustrates is that task-centred practice has the potential to highlight the power differentials between the worker and the service user. In this instance, the worker adopted an 'educator' role that, without critical analysis, could easily shift him/her into the role of 'expert'.

Termination and Evaluation

The termination stage of task-centred practice begins in the first sessions when the time limit is set and all parties are enabled to understand that the work will have an ending. Key to this termination process is the final session, which should contain an evaluation of the changes that have occurred since the initial assessment (Marsh 1997). This is done in order to remind the service user and the worker of how they perceived the problem at the onset of intervention and to evaluate what progress has been made. When carrying out this part of the work, the worker should be careful to review all the tasks, including those not completed. This process should highlight the skills and knowledge which have been used and learned through the intervention and which can be identified as having merit for future problem-solving. Such knowledge-building is as likely to apply to the worker as to the service user (Coulshed and Orme 1998). For instance, Susan learned how to negotiate with housing officials and could transfer such skills to other contexts in the future. The termination stage should be a positive session that reinforces the service user's ability to problem-solve and confirms the accomplishments that have been made during the process. Future planning, including further intervention by the worker or other agencies should also be considered in this session, potentially enabling the method to be more than a one-off activity with the service user. Indeed, it may be felt that it can be used again to deal with any additional issues that have arisen during the initial intervention. Work can continue beyond the originally agreed timescale, although this has to be organised in advance and new time limits and tasks put in place if this is considered appropriate. Caution has to be exercised, however, around how often this can be done, as the aim of the method is to encourage confidence and the development of the service user's own skills rather than dependency.

Evaluation for a task-centred method is arguably a straightforward process that involves the worker and the service user identifying whether goals have been achieved. It is this perceived clarity of outcomes that is one of the reasons for the method's acceptability in the current managerial environment. Finally, as Milner and O'Byrne (1998) highlight, for evaluation to be empowering in this method it should be a two-way process, with worker and user alike measuring the success and learning that has been achieved. Building in opportunities for workers to be evaluated by service users can provide a useful means of developing genuine partnerships and help adjust perceived power imbalances.

Issues for task-centred practice

Task-centred practice is arguably an optimistic method, moving the focus away from the person as the problem to practical and positive ways of dealing with difficulties. This is seen to build confidence because its focus is on enhancing people's capacities and strengths. It also recognises that, with support, the person with the problems also has the means to resolve them. This is reinforced by the fact that there is arguably no mystique about the way the method works. Consequently, all parties are clear about what is expected of them and why. Therefore, social work intervention should become more partnership-based as it attempts to empower users of social work services to take control over their situation, taking into account their values, beliefs and understanding (Milner and O'Byrne 1998). It is for this reason that task-centred practice is seen as being appropriate in working with ethnic-minority service users, women and other potentially oppressed groups as it facilitates and values their contribution to the process (Ahmad 1990).

Whilst it is argued that the strength of this method is its potential to facilitate empowerment and partnership, in practice this will be highly dependent on the worker and his/her approach. The task-centred method has the potential to place the needs of the worker or agency at the centre of the process rather than those of the service user. As already noted above, the role of educator in the relationship places the worker in a very powerful position, which raises a wider question about whether partnership is possible within an unequal distribution of power between worker and service user. It is also possible that this method can minimise the structural influences that are associated with many problematic situations such as unemployment, poor health, poverty, race and gender (Trevithick 2000). These are issues that need to be considered at a structural level and may be difficult for the worker, who is facing their direct local impact on the service user, to overcome. Therefore, whilst task-centred practice, as Doel (2002, p. 197) highlights, may help 'expose the subtle relationships between the different systems', to make this method empowering from a democratic perspective requires the service user to be at the heart of the process and not a product to be processed. This will be influenced by the worker's approach and consequently affect how the method is applied in practice. For example, it is possible for all the steps of this method to be followed using a procedural approach, which empowers service users at the level of informing them, but holds them to account for tasks of importance to the agency or worker. Conversely, it can be used in a way that enables service users to have a say in not just outcomes but in decision-making about how outcomes are achieved.

Concerns with the task-centred method

The task-centred method, despite its apparent simplicity, is a complex method to apply in practice. Apart from the intensive time and energy demanded of all parties to meet the time-limited goals, it also raises real concerns about sticking to these agreed tasks and goals. This is reflected in the distinction in the method about the forms of communication used within the sessions. To be successful, the worker needs to communicate with the service user in a systematic manner about the task and its implementation. However, the reality of the relationship and the fact that it is still developing means that the worker has to be responsive to what the service user has to say, including any new information (Coulshed and Orme 1998). This means that the worker constantly has to balance new information against what this means for the agreed work. Whilst the aim of the method is to be flexible and responsive in relation to the service user's situation, this can very easily become a series of steps controlled and directed by the worker who tries to stick to the initial assessment of the situation. Alternatively it can mean that the plan is repeatedly reformulated, undermining the ability to move forward. The key to achieving this balance is clearly the relevance of the initial assessment and the ability of all parties effectively to prioritise what is important and needs to be worked upon. Failure to acknowledge this complexity and the skills required, arguably, is part of the reason the method becomes confused with the completion of tasks that are a one-off activity rather than part of the process of change (Payne 1997).

A further concern of task-centred practice would be that as this method only deals with the problems that are described by the service user, it may be that there are underlying problems which are not discussed or worked with. Service users may have underlying problems that this method would not address; they may feel swamped and not have the 'emotional energy' or commitment to work on those issues (Trevithick 2000). A young person who is excluded from school on the grounds of unacceptable behaviour in class, for example, may well have a range of underlying issues related to faulty attachments, inconsistent parenting, etc. While responding to these school issues may be considered to be important in terms of the young person's stability and tasks for change could be identified, he or she may have reached such a level of anomie (Haralambos et al. 2004) that all emotional energy is taken up with resistance. As the young person can see no personal gain from the work being suggested, he or she is unlikely to have any commitment to the process. Yet, utilising a task-centred method to develop a series of tasks that build towards reintegration into the school community could offer sufficient rewards to open the door to further, more complex work later. In our experience, this method is often seen by social work students as one that is particularly helpful in building relationships with service users, thereby opening the door to other methods of intervention. Finally, despite its claims to be generic in its application, task-centred practice is less successful with families and individuals who appear subject to constant crisis (Coulshed and Orme 1998) and in situations where there is an involuntary involvement but no recognition of this by the service user (Marsh 1997). Within the context of current social work practice, this may indeed represent a considerable proportion of the people who use the service and may explain why the method is often seen as having been applied when the worker is merely carrying out practical tasks. The reality of this method is that it appears simple to implement and to fit the 'what works' performance-measurement culture but its application needs workers and service users to be organised and reflective. This is often difficult to achieve in present workplace cultures but should not stop workers from looking to utilise this method of intervention. What it does require, however, is a cognitive shift for many workers, as the task-centred method in its empowering form is proactive not reactive.

Behavioural Social Work

Behavioural work (see Figure 5.2), as with the task-centred method, is time-limited. However, it is more restricted in that it focuses on *behaviour* that is observable and changeable. In this respect it deals with surface/ presenting issues and is based on the premise that what has been learned can be unlearned (Coulshed and Orme 1998). It is a method that has a clear resonance with the 'what works?' agenda and sees itself as being scientific in its application and clear about measuring the outcomes (Hudson and Macdonald 1986; Cigno 2002). Like most social work methods, it has been adopted from related disciplines (e.g. psychology) and adapted to fit practice. The work of Hudson and Macdonald (1986) and Sheldon (1995) provide a solid starting point for understanding the method. It is able, arguably, to match social work's need for both measured outcomes and effective and ethical practice (Sheldon 1995).

Assessment ⇒ ⇒ Establishment of a baseline ⇒ ⇒ Identification of incremental ⇒ ⇒ Evaluation
for intervention   steps to modify behaviour   Measured against baseline
Specific targets for change,   Strategy for change,
e.g. use of diaries and logs   e.g. social skills training

Figure 5.2   Behavioural social work

Underpinning Theory

It was during the 1980s, largely based on the work of Goldstein (1981), that social work adopted behavioural therapy as a method when working with service users. Part of the reason for the emerging popularity of the method was its apparent ability to achieve tangible outcomes, particularly within criminal justice work (McGuire 1995). Unlike the task-centred method, behavioural work is clear about its theory base (i.e. learning theory) and what this means for any subsequent practice. Learning theory is not one but a cluster of four theories that enable the worker to study observable behaviours. These are respondent and operant conditioning, and social and cognitive learning (Payne 1997; Coulshed and Orme 1998). What they have in common is the belief that behaviour is learned and can be unlearned, although cognitive learning moves this beyond just the observable to how people make sense of their situation. It is this engagement with cognitive processes that brings the method closer to social work practice with its focus on thoughts and feelings (Sheldon 1995). The ability to unlearn behaviour or adopt new responses is important because individuals display a range of responses with which they are not happy or which are problematic in terms of the wider environment. Behavioural social work enables service users to either modify or change behaviours through a process of reinforcements both positive and negative. This is achieved by setting time-limited targets that deal with specific concerns based on a clear and concise assessment of the situation (Hudson and Macdonald 1986).

Underpinning the method is an assumption that there is an acceptable and agreed way to behave in society. This raises questions for workers about what is 'normal' and who decides this. The concern for those using the method is that this can create discriminatory practice as it can be influenced by workers' or agencies' values (Trevithick 2000). To this end, it is argued that the method's application can create an unnecessary and unhelpful power differential between the worker and the service user. This is true of early behaviourism, with its emphasis on the passive recipient of the service. However, it has become increasingly at odds with more recent applications that are more consistent with social work values of inclusion and empowerment. Sheldon and Chilvers (2000) argue that workers using behavioural intervention would only do so using informed consent and the active participation of the service user. If this is the case, the method may become more empowering as service users are involved in determining both when and how the method is utilised. It is this exchange and sharing of information that can potentially empower the service user in this method.

Assessment

Assessment is crucial for behavioural social work, as it should identify not just the causes of behaviour but how it manifests itself and what needs to be done to change it (Hudson 1994). This requires detailed investigation by the worker to obtain accurate information. The first stage of assessment and intervention is to establish the behaviours to be worked with. The emphasis will be on the present, breaking the concerning behaviour down into specific actions carried out by the service user. This is an activity that ideally should be measured to determine both the frequency and the intensity. In this respect, the method is moving beyond vague generalisations to clear statements of intent. In order to achieve this clarity, information is recorded throughout the assessment of what is happening and how often, including before, during and after the incident. This can be done through the use of dairies or written records which log more than the situation itself. When working from a more empowering perspective, the writing up and ownership of such records would be negotiated to ensure genuine partnership. How this method applies in practice can be seen in relation to operant conditioning with its ABC assessment of behaviour – antecedents, behaviour and consequences (Hudson and

Macdonald 1986; Cigno 2002). The antecedent gives the worker the opportunity to use questioning and listening skills to establish what precedes the behaviour. This can then be studied to assess how often and in what way it is manifested by the service user. The consequence is what happens immediately after the incident, and the worker should aim to discover if this is consistent, identifying how the behaviour is reinforced as perceived by the service user and significant others. Having gathered reliable and relevant information and correctly identified the problem behaviour, the worker and the service user can plan a baseline of what is happening and why, from which to proceed with the intervention.

Sandeep and Ravinder's situation provides an example of the difficulties involved in a behavioural assessment in practice. Whilst assessment can often be straightforward, with social work service users this is less often the case than one might imagine. On receiving the referral from the school, the worker was concerned to work with the family and Tarjinder on his truanting behaviour. Whilst all could acknowledge that this was the concern to be addressed, determining antecedents was a much less straightforward activity. Three interrelated areas had to be addressed and considered in relation to possible causes: Sandeep's hospitalisation, Ravinder's health and Tarjinder's experiences at school. The family and the worker had to make detailed records of what was happening in all three areas prior to any period of truancy. Whilst all three had a part to play, the worker concluded that the area of most concern was that Tarjinder was staying off school to support his mother and that this was implicitly being reinforced by Ravinder's actions. The baseline for the assessment moved from Tarjinder to his mother who was seen as providing positive, if implicit reinforcement to his truancy. This, the worker concluded, reflected Ravinder's need for support during the day, when she felt least able to cope with isolation and the demands of looking after the household. The worker then decided to work with Ravinder on building other more appropriate reinforcers, whilst reducing those that were previously being given to Tarjinder in relation to staying off school. By approaching the assessment process in this manner, the worker took account of Tarjinder's role as a young carer to both his parents and tried to set Ravinder's situation within the wider context of the structural oppression of women. Such an assessment was therefore less likely to be reinforcing this family's experience of oppression and racism.

Assessment within this method, as we have seen, is a process that should lead to the establishment of a baseline that identifies both the frequency and the intensity of the problem behaviour. In the situation highlighted above, it is apparent that this can be a complex activity to determine. However, once the intensity, frequency and duration of the problem are established, these then serve as a reference point for future action. Initial assessment aims to identify aspects of the service user's behaviour that may need to change. The baseline should identify the exact parts of the behaviour and assess their overall impact (Sheldon 1995). The worker, in collaboration with the service user and possibly significant others, then agrees a contract that specifies the target behaviour and the behavioural technique to be used in altering the behaviour. Any such contract needs not only to take account of the service user's 'story' but also to cross-reference this with other sources of information (Milner and O'Byrne 1998). It would also outline the role of the worker and the service user and how they would interact throughout the intervention. Ideally, the targets for change should focus on issues that are of priority to the service user and look to build upon positives rather than negatives, thereby attempting to create the desired behaviour with positive reinforcers rather than to punish unhelpful behaviour by negative reinforcement. As part of this process, it is important to build timescales into the process, as these are seen as encouraging and motivate the service user to complete goals. However, unlike the task-centred method, there is no specified timescale. In the main, behavioural work is seen as enabling both long-term and short-term change. For example, in criminal justice work such planned behavioural change can last from six months to a year, the length of the intervention being determined by the situation that has to be dealt with and the service user and the worker agreeing realistic time scales for this to be achieved.

When utilising behavioural methods from a progressive approach, greater emphasis is likely to be placed on the development of a secure working relationship. Service users and workers need to get to know each other to facilitate a greater understanding of the service users' sense of what is wrong and of the environment in which they are operating. During this stage, the worker should discuss any fears and concerns that the service user has and explore how the behaviour is being maintained, as well as assessing risks related to the situation.

Process of Implementation

Once the baseline has been established and all involved understand and agree on the behaviour to be changed, negotiation should take place to establish who takes on what role and task and to what effect. A programme is set up to take account of the change process so that all concerned are aware of their roles and responsibilities. The main task of this stage for the worker and the service user is to develop appropriate strategies for the targets to be achieved within agreed time limits. The texts in this area are full of suggested ways of working and many provide excellent case examples of practice (Hudson and Macdonald 1986; Hudson 1994). The strategies used in the change programme should, as far as possible, be clear and easily understood by all concerned. All of the strategies involve the worker and the service user collaborating on a series of incremental tasks or activities that will enable the service user to alter behaviours. This can be a fairly intensive involvement for the worker, who will have to consider every step of the journey in detail, ensuring that it fits the intended purpose of the intervention. Returning to the three stages discussed earlier, the focus can be on any or all three of antecedents, behaviour and consequences. The worker's role in the change programme is often seen as neutral. However, in practice this is often not the case, as he or she reinforces a service user's desired behaviour by the use of praise and positive feedback. This form of reward is most effective when given immediately, as it can lose effectiveness if it is delayed. The worker can also help to identify people and situations that provide positive reinforcement for the desired behaviour or those that maintain the problem behaviour. With Tarjinder, for example, it was important for the worker to liaise closely with the school staff to ensure that any perceived rewards he received for improving his school attendance were not then negated by inappropriate staff responses.

Ongoing evaluation and monitoring are crucial in relation to the change programme and should be carried out regularly throughout the implementation phase to ensure that all parties are reminded of the time limits (Payne 1997). As with the task-centred method, progress should be evaluated, with an emphasis on the service user's strengths, including examples of the skills that have been learned, as failure to do this means the method can quickly slip into looking for deficits and become discouraging to the service user. If the service user and the worker decide that they have not changed the behaviour, then further analysis, reassessment and intervention is required. However, if successful, then this method does not prohibit the worker and the service user looking at any other problems that need to be resolved. This can continue until all problems are managed to the user's satisfaction.

Termination and Evaluation

The structured nature of this method, with its emphasis on time limits and task review, means that termination is assumed to have been built into the process from the beginning. Given the emphasis throughout on measurement and tangible outcomes, it is interesting to note that relatively little has been written about the process of ending behavioural methods. It is assumed that situations will be resolved and that the worker will outlive their usefulness! However, given that the method also entails establishing a relationship and working alongside the service user, then endings tend not to be so straightforward in practice. The worker needs to give consideration to this part of the process, possibly tapering down the contact as the end nears. To evaluate and measure the effectiveness of the intervention, workers can refer to their original records and diaries, focusing on the target behaviour that needed to be changed. This should be a relatively straightforward activity for the worker, as the method is based on producing observable, measurable results. In terms of Tarjinder's school attendance, for example, it will either have improved or not. Evaluation at this stage relates not only to the efficacy of the intervention so far but can also consider whether future involvement would be beneficial. Termination does not necessarily mean that the change process has come to an end, as the service user may want to change something else or address another aspect of their behaviour. Having some understanding of what has changed, however, should provide a clear baseline for any future involvement.

Issues for Behavioural Work

The major strength of behavioural social work is claimed to be that it focuses on the concerns identified rather than considering the service user as the problem. Therefore, as a method it has the potential to be empowering, as it can avoid placing all of the responsibility for their situation on the service users. By defining their own problem and working in partnership with the worker, whose role is one of skilled helper, service users should feel empowered. The task-oriented and time-limited nature of the method, along with regular reviews, should enable the service user to develop problem-solving skills, confidence and autonomy. As work is time-limited, it is also possible to avoid prolonged contact with the social services and the dependence culture that is often perceived as resulting from that relationship. In addition, behavioural methods are seen as yielding results (Sheldon and Chilvers 2000), although the evidence for this might not be as strong as some state (Milner and O'Byrne 2002). Where the focus of the work is on teaching skills or correcting perceived deficits, behavioural, performance-based interventions can be particularly successful. As a method, however, it does make assumptions about the cognitive ability and willingness of the service user to participate. This therefore potentially limits its applicability. Adults with long-term mental health problems or learning disabilities are two groups of service users where the behavioural method may be less effective. For both these groups it may be that they require substantial and long-term intervention to assist them to overcome their difficulties. That said, it is a method where success can be and is measured and evaluated. This is undoubtedly a positive for both managerial and professional practice, as it can lead to workers organising and structuring their practice in a more purposeful manner. As Payne (1997) highlights, this method may appeal to service users and workers who prefer a structured and systematic approach to problems with a clear objective, as the method is predefined and the programme is measurable. Therefore, this method could be particularly helpful for inexperienced workers, as they have clear and explicit guidelines to work to and there should be no hidden agenda for the user. It is important, however, to guard against a formulaic response which over time would limit the workers' creativity.

Concerns with Behavioural Work

The concerns of this method relate not to its effectiveness but to its potential ethical implications. The fact that it concentrates on individuals' problems can be limiting if those problems are created by structural rather than personal behaviours. Unless it is underpinned by a strong anti-oppressive practice, it could end up placing responsibility for social problems such as poverty or unemployment on the service user (Trevithick 2000). In addition, the method is premised on manipulating the service users' environment, albeit with the service users' consent. This means that it is also possible to change the environment without the service users' approval, even if this is done for what are seen by the worker or the agency as 'good reasons'. This does not sit comfortably with many workers who consider it incongruent with a social work value base of self-determination and empowerment. However, as Sheldon (1995) points out, this is a potential reality for all methods, not just behavioural work. Whilst accepting this argument, it does not mean that we should ignore the worker's approach, which will directly impact on this method and the type of empowerment and partnership involved. Working from a procedural approach, workers are likely to see behavioural methods as a means of regulating service users' responses to situations and, by assuming the role of expert and following a prescribed agenda, they will assist them to achieve change. Workers from a progressive approach will be concerned that the method is dealing with the symptoms not the causes and will therefore need to look wider than the individual for any 'solution'.

Returning to the so-called 'simplicity' of the approach and its relevance to new or inexperienced workers, our experience would suggest that the devil of this method is in the detail. At a superficial level, the method has a clear logic; in practice it can become more complicated and emotionally demanding for all concerned. The assessment stage does not mean that antecedents and consequences just emerge; the complexity of these issues often needs the worker to be skilled in the field of assessment, first to see and then to make the links for the service user. Similarly, the process of implementation requires effective communication in order to enable the worker to provide the right form of reinforcer at the appropriate time. In addition, it is potentially a very time-consuming method in the short term, a factor that requires workers to be organised in order that they model characteristics such as reliability and consistency, which are central to the method (Hudson 1994).

This method, in its more empowering forms, relies on the service user being a part of the process and having the motivation to see the programme of planned change through to its conclusion, often making it difficult to apply when working with involuntary service users (Trotter 1999). Consequently, if the service user were not committed to the process, the worker would have to reassess the situation. The danger in these circumstances is that the worker may influence the service user in subtle ways when trying to fulfil policies that lead to societal, agency or workers' goals. To be empowering, the worker must be mindful not to be manipulative and remember the user's right to self-determination and empowerment. Therefore, the worker has to be careful to consult and involve the user in an open and honest way. Sharing their skills and knowledge will allow service users to see that the worker is not essential and they can use their own strengths to achieve change. To retain this approach to behavioural methods requires constant vigilance on the part of the worker as it is all too easy to drift into a more didactic worker-centred practice. An empowering approach requires more than informed consent. It is about engaging the service user in a negotiation around outcomes and the process by which they are to be achieved. Anything less risks being tokenistic or patronising.

Summary of Chapter

1. Developing a portfolio of methods is rarely a planned activity for workers in busy agency settings. However, developing good practice implies that, as far as possible, workers should look to develop the range of methods they can utilise in a systematic manner that reflects their own needs and those of the agency and the service user.

2. The task-centred and behavioural methods give emphasis to the presenting problems of service users (surface concerns) and how these can be worked on to create a more acceptable situation for service users and workers.

3. Task-centred practice is a time-limited method that gives emphasis to the service user and the worker determining a small number of areas for change that can be systematically broken down into tasks that can be completed within a three-to-four-month timescale.

4. Task-centred practice is arguably an empowering method that enables the service user to determine both the areas of concern and potential solutions. However, in reality this method is much more complex and problematic than is often presented and as a consequence can slip into being used in a technical or practical manner with service users which leaves the social worker as the expert in the relationship.

5. Behavioural methods of intervention are based on the assumption that what has been learned can be unlearned or developed. In this respect they have at times been seen to have the potential to be used by workers to manipulate service users' environments without their permission. Recent developments of these methods have stressed the importance of ethical consideration around informing and consent and consequently have found a more receptive environment amongst practitioners.

6. Both these methods have found a growing congruence with the managerial ethos and procedural approach of many social work organisations with their emphasis on outcomes. However, arguably they are less well-suited to more democratic forms of empowerment that challenge the 'expert' notion of the worker who is able to define both the situation and its solution.

6

Methods of Intervention: Working on Feelings

The two methods chosen for consideration in this chapter are the psychosocial method and crisis intervention. In contrast to the previous chapter, the emphasis here is on the impact of previous life experiences on actions and perceptions of present situations. While crisis intervention is still often claimed to be used by workers, the psychosocial method would appear to have lost its popularity in recent years. It may, however, be a bit premature to assume that this method is obsolete. Many of its constituent elements continue to be part of the practice repertoire of workers, enabling them to understand and work with those service users whose chaotic lifestyles do not seem to change, despite the extensive use of short-term methods. When discussing the potential use of the two methods, we feel it is important to consider the issue of evidencing practice. We are in no doubt that workers should as far as possible be able to justify their intervention by demonstrating its effectiveness. This activity, however, has considerable limitations for social work, as many aspects of the service do not lend themselves to measurement, the quality of relationships and feelings being two difficult areas to quantify and measure (Drummond 1993). Within this emerging culture of evidence-based practice, many social work organisations are adopting a perspective where only those aspects of work that can be quantified are seen as relevant to undertake, hence the demise of methods based on understanding and improving coping strategies. Whilst we have no desire to return to the past where practice often lacked direction and seemed purposeless, we do feel that ethical practice requires us to value the less tangible aspects of the social work task. Research with service users would suggest that this is what is valued by service users, who comment that the worker's attitude and understanding was the key to their process of change (NISW 1996). It is for this reason that we feel we should not write off psychosocial methods, but be cautious in their application, relating them in an empowering framework that genuinely considers the social as well as the psychological.

Psychosocial Casework

Psychosocial casework (see Figure 6.1) is a method of intervention where the professional relationship is used over time to provide the opportunity to increase service users' understanding and to enable them to develop more effective ways of coping. The premise is that through understanding how people negotiate and manage their external environment we are able to obtain insight into how their personalities have developed. The context within which this understanding and explanation is developed is one where, with the worker's support, service users can safely examine past experiences. While other methods may focus more on presenting problems, psychosocial methods tend to be more concerned with their often powerful antecedents. It is concerned with the pace at which service users can adjust their thoughts and feelings and therefore tends not to be time-limited. Psychosocial casework has a long tradition in social work, dating back to the writings of Mary Richmond (1922) and Florence Hollis (1964, 1972). Hollis's work in particular provides a useful starting point for the method, highlighting the importance of both the psychological and sociological factors and their interrelationship in its utilisation. Her work challenges one of the main criticisms of the method, and a reason for its decreasing popularity, that it overemphasises the psychological at the expense of the social. As Hollis (1972, p. 9) states: 'Casework has always been a psychosocial treatment method. It recognises the interplay of both internal psychological and external social causes of dysfunctioning and endeavors to enable the individual to meet his needs more fully and to function more adequately in his social relationships.'

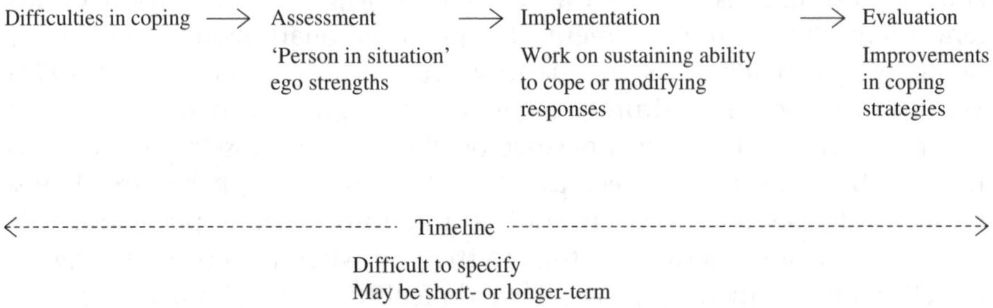

Difficulties in coping $\longrightarrow$ Assessment $\longrightarrow$ Implementation $\longrightarrow$ Evaluation

| | 'Person in situation' ego strengths | Work on sustaining ability to cope or modifying responses | Improvements in coping strategies |

$\longleftarrow$------------------------------------ Timeline --$\longrightarrow$

Difficult to specify
May be short- or longer-term

Figure 6.1   Psychosocial casework

Underpinning Theory

At the heart of psychosocial casework is the need for the worker to understand how the external pressures – *press* – and internal responses – *stress* – interact and impinge on the service user's responses in any given situation (Hollis 1972, p. 10). What this method offers workers is a way of understanding service users and why they act as they do, and the interconnections between internal and external environments. The method does have a distinct theoretical framework based on personality development that emphasises the individuals' ability to make sense of and change the problems they face in their lives. Important concepts for this theory include:

- the influence of the past on the present
- defence mechanisms
- the unconscious and its influence on shaping our actions and responses.

Whilst the worker's approach will give emphasis to different explanations for each of these areas, concerns for the service user in this method are seen as having their origins in past experiences, particularly those related to attachment, detachment and loss. These may restrict the service users' ability to create positive relationships, personally or in relation to their environment (Howe 1995; Milner and O'Byrne 1998). Difficulties occur as individuals are unable to negotiate a favourable balance of the competing demands across the life stages with inappropriate responses being developed and repeated at points in later life. Returning to the work of Hollis (1972), she considered that personality theory was based on Freudian principles with its unconscious mental tensions and friction between the id, superego and ego. The id represents the individual's hedonistic desire for the pursuit of pleasure, while the superego attempts to restrict this by the introduction of moral precepts. This leaves the ego as the arbitrator between the inner and outer world, attempting to negotiate 'socially acceptable' solutions. When such arbitration is unsuccessful, the individual can become emotionally 'stuck', resulting in problems later in development (Coulshed and Orme 1998). Perceiving itself to be under threat, the personality then constructs defence mechanisms including denial, projection, intellectualisation and transference (Payne 1997). It is important to note that all individuals have defence mechanisms developed in the past to make sense of the world they inhabit. They may not, however, be working to the strategic advantage of the individual, and part of the skill of the worker in this situation is to assist with the development of more appropriate coping strategies. With Brian, for example, his use of alcohol and violent responses to difficult situations could have been coping strategies he had developed to defend himself against inner pain. Working with him might well involve anger

management as a strategic short-term response until he was able to con-
template working on these inner feelings utilising a psychosocial
method. Using the worker/service user relationship as the main medium
of change might enable Brian to achieve the necessary level of insight
and the impetus for change.

Central to this method is making an appropriate assessment of the
service users' ego strengths in order for them to determine whether they
can cope with the stress or anxiety aroused by intervention (Coulshed
and Orme 1998). It is also intended that this will provide insight into
how the worker will shape the basis of intervention. For example, if the
individual is not ready to deal with internal issues, the emphasis on
change may then move to the environment. Crucial to this analysis is
that service users may be unaware of their responses or why they have
developed, as their reactions are being motivated at an unconscious level.
This implies that issues cannot always be taken at face value. Workers also
need to have a good level of self-awareness so that they do not use their
own defences to avoid challenging situations with which they are
uncomfortable or are unconsciously trying to avoid. In this respect, effective psychosocial work relies upon workers obtaining supervision that
challenges not just their thinking but also their actions (Hawkins and
Shohet 2000).

Assessment

Assessment emphasises understanding the *person in situation* (Hollis 1972,
p. 10), which requires a systematic and thorough analysis of these 'outer'
and 'inner' worlds (Howe 2002). The process of assessment according to
Hollis (1972, p. 260–1) consists of 'trying to understand, first, what the
problem is; second, what seems to be contributing to the trouble; and,
third, what can be changed and modified'. Central to this process is establishing a relationship between the service user and the worker that is
based on trust and understanding. This enables service users to explore in
a positive environment those issues in their past and present that are
impacting on their world. Concern about probing into these areas often
creates anxiety for students, who feel they have to delve into parts of the
service users' past which are not relevant (Jacobs 1994). It is important to
note at this stage that not all formative experiences occur in childhood or
are unconscious. In effect, assessment is about making the appropriate
connections rather than indiscriminately trawling for all information
about the past.

John, whom we met in Chapter 2, provides an example of assessing what are relevant formative experiences in the present situation. His early childhood would appear to have been 'normal', although John felt that he was an essentially shy child. However, in his mid-teens through to his twenties, his work as a professional sportsman meant that he was a constant source of attention and occasionally adulation. This continued into his later working life and marriage, where he was able to hold prominent and high-profile positions in both his employment and his social activities. John's self-esteem had continued to be supported by the relationship with his partner who, in his own words, had 'pampered' him. More recently, John had suffered a number of significant losses – the death of his partner, his retirement from paid work, changes in his social activities – which had reduced his ability to problem-solve independently. His sense of isolation and his limited social network had led him to make regular use of social work services. Therefore, for John it had been mid- and later-life experiences that were more pertinent in relation to his behaviour not, as a more rigid application of the psychosocial method would suggest, his early life experiences.

The worker's role in this process is to create a relationship that is nurturing and enabling for the service user. This may encourage an element of dependency on the part of service users that can be a positive platform from which to begin safely to explore areas of concern. The assessment process is not curtailed by time constraints, as this would negate the therapeutic element of the method. Timing will be dependent on the pace of the service user, so this could allow for a brief and in-depth form of intervention as much as it could a lengthy, comprehensive period. This poses the challenge for the worker of considering what areas the service user has the ego strength to address and what needs to be worked on at a later stage. Further, it opens up the question of service users' participation in terms of their readiness or understanding to work in partnership in these choices. Once problems have been agreed, a plan of action should be developed that will help service users to move on in their lives. To be empowering, the assessment should also consider the service users' perception of events, their self-image and their coping mechanisms and, as far as possible, involve them in the decision-making process. This requires taking account of factors such as race, gender, disability, etc., if the worker is to maintain an anti-oppressive approach.

Intervention

Having assessed the situation, the next step is to identify the appropriate techniques to enable the service user to change. Unlike other methods, however, it is difficult using the psychosocial method to provide a template or framework to follow in all circumstances, as the solution for service users will be unique to them and their experiences. That said, Hollis (1972, p. 78) identifies six techniques that can be utilised within psychosocial methods. Coulshed and Orme (1998, p. 146–9) suggest that two of these techniques are helpful to the worker and service user in working towards their goals; *sustaining* and *modifying*.

The *sustaining* technique is where workers show an interest in the service users' situation, offering emotional and practical support in terms of their ongoing relationship. In essence, they are using their relationship to provide a safe environment for service users to talk, think, reflect and plan more relevant responses to their situation. As Coulshed and Orme (1998) identify, this can be done using a variety of techniques, including ventilation, realistic reassurance, acceptance, logical discussion, role-modelling, giving information, offering advice and guidance, and environmental manipulation. With support, acceptance, advice and guidance from the worker, service users should feel more confident and motivated to challenge the causes of their situation both cognitively and practically. From this brief outline it is apparent that sustaining is a 'talking' remedy which requires good communication skills on the part of the worker, both verbal and non-verbal. The worker needs to be aware of the depth of the service user's difficulties and the limitations of his/her own skills, as deeper psychiatric concerns should not be tackled using this method. While it may have therapeutic aspects, it is important to guard against dealing with issues that may require different specialised help.

Modifying procedures tend to be more challenging of the service users' perceptions of themselves and their world. However, similar to sustaining techniques, these are designed to enable service users to develop their ego strengths and subsequently their ability to cope with the outside pressures they face. This will hopefully enable service users to gain greater awareness of and insight into previously unrecognised strengths in their personality (Howe 2002). Using modifying procedures, the worker would be attempting to do a number of things, including using reflective communication to widen the service user's self-awareness; confrontation to highlight patterns of feeling and thinking, and clarification to link the past to the present. The choice of modifying or sustaining and what techniques will be used to support them is dependent on the service user's situation and ego strengths. There is no formulaic solution that can be determined in advance of action as this will be dependent on the service users and their coping abilities. However, no matter what techniques are employed, the intention is the same: to enable service users to develop an understanding of where the behaviour has originated, the defence mechanisms they employ and the building blocks that can enable them to move on.

Returning to John's situation, the worker enabled him to ventilate his feelings about how he felt and was now viewed by society, enabling him to unburden the feeling of no longer having worth or importance. The worker also attempted to confront him about the present pattern of responses and its limited relevance in meeting his needs in a positive way. Using these techniques and information supplied by the worker, John was able to think about why he had responded as he had and how he might be able to find ways of building his social networks. John started to look for challenges within relevant community organisations that represented his interests and where he felt he could make a contribution.

This method of working often takes time, as small changes can usually only be contemplated as the service users' ego strength develops and enables them to move on to new challenges or goals. In John's case, the work took several months of regular visits, enabling him slowly to explore his feelings about his losses and bereavement and to put his present actions into a working perspective. Whilst the aim of intervention is positive change, it also acknowledges that this may not always be a straightforward process. Service users can become stuck or regress and what is required is support from the worker to enable them to move forward. Whilst this may sound a very complex way of working, its practical application is often much easier to undertake and follow. For example, a specific psychosocial tool used by many workers is that of the 'life story book' (Ryan 1993). This is used to help service users to understand where they have come from and how events within their lives have influenced the way they feel and behave. The techniques of sustaining and modifying can be utilised in the process of life-story work. During the sustaining phase, workers may create opportunities for service users to deconstruct past events in order to ventilate feelings that may have been previously suppressed. This may also involve a degree of reassurance and information-giving in an attempt to redress previously inaccurate perceptions of past events. By developing a more realistic appraisal of past events, service users can then be encouraged to modify aspects of their behaviour that may be perceived as problematic. Therefore, whilst this method has been seen as a 'talking' remedy, this does not preclude the worker from undertaking practical activities or tasks. However, practical tasks are not the main focus of the work, but a means to an end.

Termination and Evaluation

Termination within this method and process has no set timescale and is rarely discussed from the start of contact. This is because the nature of the method is about service users obtaining personal insight and change, factors, as we have seen above, which have the potential to create regression or periods of being stuck and which require ongoing worker support. However, endings should be discussed with the service user on an ongoing basis so that they are not a shock to personal functioning or support networks. It is also envisaged that the ending phase will be characterised by extending time between sessions as service users take greater control over their lives (Stepney and Ford 2000). Central to this method is the service user, so endings are not about the worker or agency. If the work needs to be extended, therefore, it should be possible for this to happen. Evaluation is also a problematic activity for the psychosocial method as there is no built-in framework or timescale, as intervention is very much an ongoing process. This lack of a final evaluation point makes the termination of this method difficult, as it becomes hard for either the worker or the service user to be able to identify when the intervention is complete (Coulshed and Orme 1998). Unlike the task-centred method or behavioural work, the goals tend to be less concrete, which means that progress for the service user is more difficult to judge. Therefore, whilst it is not impossible to build evaluation and termination into the method, these aspects are not given much attention in the literature. It tends to reflect an 'expert' rather than a negotiated approach to the work. However, building in review dates with the service user where the progress and future plans can be discussed has the potential to make this method more empowering and partnership-orientated.

Issues for Psychosocial Casework

The central issue for this method is how empowering it can be, given its emphasis on the worker as the 'expert'. The traditional literature on the psychosocial method undoubtedly gives the worker considerable power and control over the passive service user, as the emphasis is on the worker interpreting what is important in both past and present (Hollis 1972; Coulshed and Orme 1998). In addition, the worker determines whether the service user is able to cope with issues or not, a powerful role to hold and one that makes partnership a difficult goal to achieve. It is this assumed limited ability of service users to define their own issues that is at the core of the empowerment debate within psychosocial work. Arguably, the power imbalance means that, at best, empowerment is at the level of informing rather than genuine partnership. The danger of this 'elitist' stance (Trevithick 2000) is that, unless the worker's value base is anti-oppressive, it can be used to reinforce social inequalities around issues such as race and gender. For example, Dominelli (1991) questions the ability of white workers to understand or empathise with the racist context that impacts on black people's lives. These concerns would suggest that a psychosocial method would be complex if not impossible between a black service user and a white worker. Whilst proponents of the method in recent years have tried to respond to these issues, they have difficulty including the issue of structural oppression within the method's rationale. This means its application often minimises issues such as poverty and oppression. In this situation it is all too easy for workers to adopt the role of 'fixer' (Howe 1987).

Probably the biggest issue for the psychosocial method is its relevance in the present 'what works' and managerial environment. As already discussed, many of the more recent methods are reactions to the perceived ineffectiveness of longer-term, open-ended methods such as psychosocial work, with its rather subjective measurement of success. In this respect, the method has very little resonance with a culture concerned with value for money and with the short-term justification of the use of scarce resources. Arguably, this method is focused on providing a service that matches the needs of service users, no matter how expansive or vague. In this respect, it may be out of touch with the culture and level of service that many agencies seek to develop. That said, it would be remiss to ignore the positives that the method brings to practice. Workers frequently use elements of the psychosocial method to make sense of the situations that they and service users face in their daily practice. They often consider past influences in order to make sense of present situations; they are aware that people use defence mechanisms to enable them to cope appropriately in given circumstances and understand that people are not always aware of what motivates others or themselves. It also provides a forum for service users to talk about their issues; it acknowledges them as unique individuals and enables them to feel safe to express their fears and concerns in an unhurried atmosphere. This also holds true for workers within appropriate supervision, as they can reflect on their own practice and any possible hidden agendas and assumptions. This leads to the main strength claimed by the psychosocial method that, by building an appropriate relationship, the worker and the service user will challenge the underlying problems, potentially preventing the continual return of service users to social work agencies. It is much easier to envisage the appeal of this method within an individual pathology approach that seeks to individualise problems and concerns. The challenge for workers, however, is how to utilise this method within a practice that identifies the importance of structural factors, i.e. a progressive approach.

Concerns with the Psychosocial Method

A major concern with the method, for those who wish to use it in an empowering manner, is that traditional theorists and practitioners have adopted an individual pathology approach. This tends to emphasise the individual as needing expert help owing to their limited understanding and current capabilities, thus ignoring structural oppression and the influence this can have on any situation. This potential for 'victim-blaming' can occur even when the method does consider the social dimension, as it tends to adopt functionalist systems theory with its tendency to mould individual behaviour to meet more socially acceptable norms. This is not to suggest, however, that more progressive approaches cannot be utilised to develop this aspect of the method. This evolving understanding has seen the method move away from notions of worker expertise, which have previously influenced the relationship with the service user, to a more open and sharing perceptive. Despite these attempts to develop the method in a more critical fashion, putting this into practice has proved more difficult to achieve. The method has an inbuilt power differential between worker and service user that is problematic to overcome as service users are assumed to have limited insight and understanding of why they react and behave the way they do. That said, no matter what the workers' approach, essentially their role in this method is to provide a safe and nurturing environment in which the service user can reflect upon, challenge and change responses that they currently find problematic (Howe 2002).

Crisis Intervention

Crisis intervention is a method that was developed by American psychiatrists (Lindemann 1944; Caplan 1964; Rapoport 1970) and obtained popularity within social work from the early 1970s onwards (Payne 1997). It is a short-term method based on the premise that people develop coping mechanisms which can be disrupted by changes that precipitate a crisis in their lives (Thompson 1991). Whilst a crisis has the potential to harm or disrupt, it also provides an opportunity and the motivation for change. Service users, with appropriate support, can learn new ways of dealing with situations and develop more effective coping mechanisms. It is this orientation towards the future that is the key to the method's aims and application, providing those in crisis with the drive and direction to resolve their situation. Whilst the original texts on the method have a strong medical orientation, the work of O'Hagan (1986) and Thompson (1991) is more accessible from a social work perspective, the latter in particular bridging the method's underpinning theory to anti-oppressive practice.

Underpinning Theory

Crisis intervention (see Figure 6.2) emerged as a means of understanding the human condition in 1944 when Eric Lindemann wrote about the aftermath

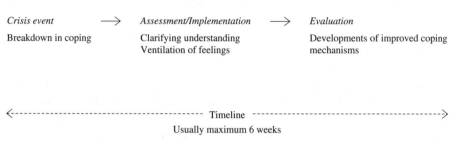

Figure 6.2 Crisis intervention

of the 1942 Coconut Grove fire in Boston (Lindemann 1944). While investigating the aftermath of what was at the time the single biggest loss of life in an American incident, he established that while some people recovered fairly quickly, others remained psychologically affected. His investigations, later extended by Caplan (1964), indicated that the process of recovery was affected by a number of factors including the ego-integrity of the individuals concerned. From this work, the theory of crisis emerged. In its initial form, it was based very much around a medical model, focusing on the physiological impact of sudden change. This emphasised the importance of the 'fight or flight' response in humans that can be utilised as a source of energy or can so overwhelm the individual as to be immobilising. How individuals respond to the same stimuli will be affected by many factors, including their own cognitive appraisal of the event itself, their existing coping strengths and their support structures (Aquilera 1998).

Hence when we look at the classic literature, crisis is seen as 'an upset in a steady state' (Rapoport 1970) or 'disequilibrium' in the service user's situation (Caplan 1964). Crisis, therefore, becomes a personal issue for which service users are responsible owing to their own limitations. More recent attempts to develop crisis intervention have moved on from this early approach and have begun to consider issues such as poverty and gender, adding an anti-oppressive perspective to the method. Thompson (1991), for example, uses social learning theory (Bandura 1971) for the psychological base and, in terms of sociology, moves away from consensus to emphasise the potential for conflict and oppression to arise. What is common to all perspectives is the belief that people face points in their lives where they can become immobilised by new situations or significant events. While such situations can be construed as threatening to the wellbeing of the individual, crisis theorists would also see such events as potentially positive. In terms of crisis theory, they can potentially provide the context for personal development, as service users are more open to help from the worker and significant others. The goal of the worker's intervention would then be to enable service users to develop new coping skills to ensure that they were able to deal with situations more effectively.

One of the main difficulties with the method is defining what is meant by 'crisis' and applying it to practice. In its common usage, crisis is usually related to situations of high drama and important decisions with significant consequences. Unfortunately for many workers, this is how they interpret the notion of crisis, seeing it as based around having to deal with emergencies. In this respect they may be defining and applying *crisis* in relation to their own or agencies' needs rather than those of service users. Crisis intervention is not about a type of organisational response to workplace pressure but a method of intervention related to the service user's needs (Thompson 2000). It is also about more than struggling to cope with the stresses that everyday life creates or the ongoing chaotic situations that some service users appear to face. Stress is experienced as a natural part of the human condition. However, most people adapt by using new or different coping mechanisms. It is only when these strategies do not work that people can find themselves in a situation that they cannot resolve and they may be considered to be 'in crisis' (Coulshed and Orme 1998). The level at which this occurs and the way it is manifested will be dependent on the individual and his/her previous life experiences and socialisation. There are, therefore, no checklists or formulaic responses that come to the aid of workers. Each person's experience is unique and therefore merits a unique response.

> For example, Brian, as we saw in Chapter 3, had been struggling to cope with his world, enduring many stressful events, including appearing in court and being placed on probation, living in poverty and facing threats to the security of his accommodation. Whilst these were significant stress factors, none could be said to have precipitated a crisis in his coping ability. However, three months into his probation order, Brian overslept and failed to attend one of his regular meetings with his probation worker. Hardly a high-drama event. However, for Brian its impact was to create a sense of hopelessness about how his life was progressing and who he wanted to be, which was not an offender involved in the criminal justice system. His response was to become withdrawn and less communicative, feeling that he was incapable of doing anything properly, including getting out of bed. Whilst this was a far cry from what would be considered a traditional crisis situation, it was picked up by the worker, who recognised the significance for Brian. By sensitively exploring with Brian how he was feeling, the worker was able to help him identify the key elements of his life that he was now motivated to change. This provided additional energy and focus for the work being undertaken through his probation order. This is not to argue that all crises lack drama or risk, but to highlight that a crisis can also be more subtle in its signs and difficult for the worker to pick up in practice.

However, O'Hagan (1986) highlights the fact that workers are frequently faced with the more high-profile forms of crisis, often around new work with service users whose situations can be of a fairly concerning and threatening nature. Consequently, he argues that crisis work should only be undertaken by experienced workers with appropriate systems of supervision. Thompson (1991), whilst accepting this reality, argues that crisis can also occur at any point in time when working with a service user. In this context, the main aim of the worker, as Thompson (1991, p. 24) points out, is to 'teach new and better coping skills or facilitate in whatever ways possible the development of these'.

Whilst each crisis and its causes and consequences will be unique to the service user's situation, this does not mean that the method provides no guidance in relation to the process or nature of crisis itself. It is clearly premised that crises are brought about by a *precipitant event* that upsets normal coping mechanisms, thereby creating a series of reactions in the service user, which will in turn influence the worker's response and action. Caplan (1964) identifies the three phases of crisis as 'impact', 'recoil' and 'adjustment and adaptation' (Thompson 1991, p. 10). The impact phase reflects the service users' initial reactions to the precipitant event, when they experience feelings of disbelief about their current situation. In this context, normal coping mechanisms are utilised, but their failure often means that service users' stress levels rise and they feel unable to change their situation. Characteristic of this phase is a feeling of being lost or of disbelief as service users struggle to make sense of why their usual responses are failing to work. These initial experiences are quickly followed by the 'recoil' phase, which is usually characterised by strong feelings that can be directed towards the self, to others or to both. The inability of individuals to solve problems in their usual way can lead to frustration and confusion. Tension then increases, creating feelings of fear and anxiety for the service user and once again building on their feelings of helplessness and disorientation (O'Hagan 1986). It is important to remember that while this is related to *affect*, it can also create *effect* in which physical symptoms such as tiredness and nausea may appear. The final phase is that of adjustment and adaptation, which Thompson (1991, p. 10) describes as 'breakthrough or breakdown', as this will determine the success or failure of the crisis intervention. If unresolved, the tension can mount until the person reaches breaking-point, which can lead to another crisis situation for the individual concerned. However, it is the tension and energy associated with crisis that gives this stage the potential for change, making service users more accepting of developing new ways of working and thinking as they strive to restore equilibrium to their world. Fundamental to this method is the notion that crises are time-limited and that this sets restrictions for the worker and the service user to effect an acceptable way of coping. Whilst the time limit varies, depending on which theorist you read, it would be fair to say that it would require a six-week period (Caplan 1964) for the work to have a chance of success.

Throughout these phases, the worker can be in a very powerful position, intervening with someone who is emotionally vulnerable. In this context, it is important that workers do not encourage dependency or inappropriately use their power to define solutions. While the worker may provide safety and structure, it is service users who should determine what the crisis is for them and how they would wish to cope in the future. This potential to disempower means that it is important for the notion of partnership and empowerment to be introduced into the intervention at the earliest juncture, with both the worker and the service user assessing what has happened, why and the potential solutions. That said, this is often difficult, as service users feel unable to act or are looking to workers for solutions.

Assessment

Unlike most other methods, it is difficult to separate out the assessment and implementation stages in crisis intervention. Early assessment of each situation is important to ensure that unhelpful coping skills do not come to the fore in the 'adjustment and adaptation' phase. Of necessity, workers will often be planning ways forward with service users, based on limited information that will evolve as the intervention proceeds. In this respect, assessment and implementation are often intertwined, as opposed to separate and distinct stages. Given the future orientation of the method, assessment is not about emphasising precipitant events or what went wrong. It is more about clarifying service users' understanding of the event; how they feel about that; what coping mechanisms have been successfully used in the past. Workers should also be considering wider support networks, including their own time and energy, and how they can be utilised to positive effect. This should incorporate the service users' perception of strengths. In essence, what workers are looking for in their assessment is a mixture of understanding of the coping ability and strengths of service users and the influence of structural factors, and how these can be used to empower rather than oppress. The aim of this is to enable the identification of a limited number of short-term goals that can be positively worked upon and which, as far as possible, can help bring understanding to a situation and prevent further deterioration in the service user (Coulshed and Orme 1998). These steps should also be flexible enough to reflect the changing situation that surrounds the service user. Helping service users to resume control of their lives at a time when their self-esteem is low and their motivation limited is a task that requires skill and patience. As a part of this activity, the worker can look at the ventilation of feelings and practical tasks that will enable the service user to gain confidence and obtain a more positive self-image.

Of particular importance in the assessment process is that the worker should be aware of the service users' 'social location', including issues such as class, gender, age, culture, race and sexual orientation. The nature of the service users' vulnerable situation means that it would be easy for workers to impose their world-view and have the power to ensure that this prevailed. The need to consider wider structural issues is emphasised by Thompson (1991), who points out how racism can be seen as a contributory factor in the onset of crisis and the stresses and pressures it brings to bear. Similarly, inequalities based on gender place an increased burden of coping on women who may be more vulnerable to crisis owing to the oppressive nature of a society based on sexism. Therefore, workers need to be aware of these influences and practise in a way that does not reinforce or add to the already oppressive situation faced by many service users.

Finally, during assessment and the implementation stage workers need to adopt a positive attitude to the task, providing service users with optimism for the future through reframing as a counterbalance to their present feelings of anxiety and hopelessness. Alongside this is the need for workers to be 'calming and being calm', thereby not adding to the tension of the situation (Thompson 1991, p. 40). This includes not only being calm with the person in crisis, but also being calm themselves in order that they do not add to the crisis but create an environment that is safe and helps to develop solutions that are achievable by the service user.

Implementation

The time-limited nature of this method means that intervention needs to be planned carefully and follow a logic that works for the individual service user. Once the area of work has been identified, the worker's role is to help maintain focus and enable the service user to progress the task. The method utilises a range of techniques including keeping the situation real (confronting), enabling the service user to talk about his/her feelings (ventilation) and provide practical support (task management) (Thompson 2000). The aim of these techniques is to keep the situation positive and meaningful for the service user in order that he/she can begin to develop helpful coping mechanisms that build his/her self-esteem. This is reinforced by the time limits set, which are designed to continue to motivate both worker and service user. Maintaining the momentum can be challenging for workers, particularly in the early stages when service users struggle to find motivation for change. There is a potential for workers to adopt a more proactive role, with the inevitable concerns around dependency. This may encourage the service user to see the situation as more easily resolved by an 'expert' outsider, which again may impact on self-esteem.

Given the dynamic nature of the process of intervention, assessment remains an ongoing feature of the method. Information, and how it is understood, changes as the service user responds to the support being offered. This, however, should not lead workers to become complacent about what has been achieved. Service users in crisis can be unpredictable and at times very self-absorbed. In more extreme forms, service users may have intense feelings of self-harm or a desire to harm others. Constant vigilance is necessary to ensure the safety of both the service user and the worker in such circumstances (Roberts 2000). Whilst any method of intervention requires that we re-evaluate our assessment and action, this is particularly important in crisis intervention, as increasing levels of understanding will mean the need constantly to review aims and actions. As service users begin to make greater sense of what precipitated the crisis, so they increase confidence in their capacity to problem-solve and develop their coping strategies. This process can be encouraged by the worker reflecting back past events and allowing the service user to identify changes, however small.

Overall, the role of the worker during the intervention phases will be to enable service users to identify what has worked in attempting to solve the problems in the past and present. Key to this activity is incremental goal-setting that should be encouraged from the outset. This provides a focus for service users and enables them to have positive experiences in their present negative situation. In this context, it is important that workers, working on tasks in a positive and supportive manner, provide a template for future actions. Crisis intervention as a method is demanding both emotionally and practically for workers and should not be considered unless their resources and those of the agency make this possible. Whilst the literature does not prescribe the number of visits, our experience would suggest that this method could, in some instances, imply daily contact. Whilst this is not the norm, in high-risk situations contact will be regular and intense to enable support and direction to be there at the right time for the service user.

Termination and Evaluation

Termination is an important part of intervention and is built into this method from its inception. Clearly, when utilising a method where the worker's role is pivotal, the process of terminating involvement needs to be carefully planned. Any crisis situation, by definition, has a natural time span within which the motivation for change is optimal. Prolonging contact beyond the point where it is constructive runs the risk of a dependent relationship emerging. As part of the intervention process, service users have been encouraged to respond to focused time limits. Therefore, as part of this method it is important periodically to remind service users of the time remaining so that they can start to think about once again coping on their own. Any abrupt termination can undo all that has been achieved during the intervention and risks precipitating further crises (Thompson 1991). The formal ending stage (termination) should take place in the last one or two interviews and should involve reviewing and evaluating what has been achieved, what new coping mechanisms have been developed and how they have been used throughout the work (Coulshed and Orme 1998).

Evaluating how successful crisis intervention has been can be a complex process. It is a future-oriented method, making the immediate benefits difficult to assess. In addition, it is about developing coping mechanisms that are by their nature intangible and about emotions/feelings. However, there are a number of advantages when using this method of intervention. If it is successful and the service user has developed new coping mechanisms, the need for social work intervention in the future is potentially minimised. It is therefore economical in terms of further resources and workers' time, despite the resource-intensive initial stages.

Issues for Crisis Intervention

Crisis intervention, with its future-orientated focus, is seen as both preventative and effective in enabling people to develop better coping mechanisms. This time-limited intervention retains a currency and apparent relevance in the increasingly pressured context of social work service delivery. Our view would be that using this method within the context of agency service provision requires a structured system of supervision and support for workers. It is also resource-intensive in terms of workers' time and emotional energy. Appropriate 'self-care' for workers is therefore vital. Arguably, it is for these reasons that it has become less congruent with the present social work environment with its emphasis on 'value for money'. The difficulty of this situation is that crises continue to occur for many service users and, unless addressed appropriately, will lead to increased pressure on the service itself.

Concerns with Crisis Intervention

Probably the most concerning aspect of crisis intervention is its potential to be used in a disempowering manner with service users. The nature of the method means that there is always the danger of the worker moving into formal 'expert' mode. This is a situation that sits comfortably with the original application of the method, which Thompson (1991, p. 13) highlights has the potential to place 'overemphasis on "internal" psychological coping resources', limiting the importance of social networks and supports and consideration of the issue of oppression. This tends to reinforce the inherent power imbalance between the worker and the service user. In this respect, the method lends itself to approaches that diminish the importance of power and conflict, particularly from a structural perspective. Arguably, the method fits much easier with the limited form of individual rather than democratic empowerment. Crisis intervention has a congruence with the individual pathology approach with its emphasis on the role of the worker and also the importance it places on the psychological. Solution-focused therapy is an example of how the basic tenets of this method can be applied in a more empowering manner, taking account of the service user's narrative (Aquilera 1998). Should workers wish to utilise this more empowering practice, they will need to be constantly aware of the power they hold in a crisis situation and how abuse of power can easily occur when dealing with vulnerable service users. Therefore, an understanding of social disadvantages and discrimination is necessary in the daily work with people in crisis situations to make this method not just effective but ethical.

Summary of Chapter

1. Whilst both these methods consider underlying/depth concerns of the situation, psychosocial casework tends to be long-term, looking at the general influence of past events whilst crisis intervention is much more short-term, looking at specific life events and how these impact on coping mechanisms.

2. Psychosocial casework is based on the premise that the worker, over time and through the utilisation of the professional relationship, will enable service users to increase their understanding and develop more effective ways of coping. It is through this process that service users can safely examine past experiences and gain insight into how their personality has developed and what needs to be done to adapt more acceptable responses and actions.

3. Crisis intervention, on the other hand, is more concerned with how coping mechanisms are no longer able to work for service users in terms of the demands of their present situation. The worker in this situation enables the service user to consider what coping mechanisms have

worked in the past and how these can be built upon to develop new and relevant strategies for the present. Key to this method is that when coping mechanisms fail, this leads to a time-limited period, usually around six weeks, where the service user is motivated to change and adopt a new way of living.

4. Both these depth methods have found it difficult to establish themselves in modern social work organisations with their emphasis on outcome and clarity of intervention. Psychosocial casework, in particular, appears to have become marginalised as its open-ended commitment to work with service users is at variance with the growing 'what works' agenda. In addition, both methods lend themselves to 'expert' workers defining the problem owing to their greater experience and insight, factors that are at variance with the democratic empowerment agenda in relation to service users.

5. Different methods of intervention have different focuses, aims and objectives that will influence what can be achieved by any intervention. In addition, the ability to use the method in an empowering manner, whilst possible for all methods, is clearly influenced by their underpinning assumptions and the worker's approach.

7

Selecting Methods

Methods of social work intervention, as has been discussed in previous chapters, are the main means by which workers manage the process of work over time, providing structure and purpose for all involved. To utilise methods, workers need to be clear about their strategic response to the needs of service users, both expressed and implicit, in order to plan and intervene appropriately. Selecting a method of intervention is therefore more than a mere technical process of information-gathering and form-filling to achieve a desired outcome. As Milner and O'Byrne (2002) acknowledge, it requires synthesising the analysis and understanding of the service user and the worker with the mandate of the agency providing the service. Therefore, methods of intervention take place within a context that constrains and confines the available options and is rarely straightforward. Through negotiation, the competing demands of all parties must be considered and the basis for anti-oppressive practice established. This is rarely a simple activity, as the boundaries between perspectives are often not fully articulated. For example, the control requirement of the criminal justice process may at first glance be entirely at odds with the welfare aspirations of the worker, yet both perspectives are likely to be implicit in the discussion with the service user when deciding upon an appropriate method of intervention. Nevertheless, workable plans have to be developed if change is to occur for service users and the selection of an appropriate method can often be the key to ensuring co-operation and participation.

Using methods moves the social work task from a 'commonsense' activity to a thinking, reflecting and doing activity influenced and directed by the choice and application of theory to practice. Methods are not theory or value-free; they are based on assumptions about the service user and wider society. In addition, they will be influenced by our approach, particularly in relation to the type of partnership and empowerment that is employed. Effective and ethical practice implies that selecting a method requires us to have a sound understanding of a range of methods of intervention. This does not mean a dogged adherence to one particular method in the face of evidence suggesting its limited effectiveness. Nor does it imply a 'pick and mix' approach, hoping that at least one will yield some success. Rather, we need to draw upon a mixture of experience, research and practice wisdom that is shared with the service user in order that all parties can agree which methods are most appropriate to the context of the work being undertaken.

Selecting a method of intervention is, therefore, a complex process, as workers are often dealing with uncertainty in the service user's world and the worker's situation. In addition, no two people are the same; different service users have different capabilities, levels of confidence and support. This means that there is rarely one ideal method for a given situation, but a range of alternatives that have advantages and disadvantages to their utilisation. Therefore, workers, as Trevithick (2000, p. 1) points out, need to have 'a tool-box of interventions and a sound theoretical and research base from which to begin to understand people'. The reality for many workers, however, is that they rarely have the expertise to use all the methods available (Marsh and Triseliotis 1996). Workers do not need to have mastered all the methods, but do need to work constantly at widening the range of options at their disposal, thereby enabling them to respond flexibly and appropriately to each new situation (Parker and Bradley 2003). Given the uniqueness of each situation, workers need to recognise when one method is appropriate and when the circumstances need a more flexible response, utilising a range of methods. Flexibility, however, as Marsh and Triseliotis (1996) identified in their study of newly qualified practitioners, creates difficulties and dilemmas about what method or methods can be utilised in any given situation. This is not an easy issue to resolve, as most methods provide potential solutions to a range of situations but by definition also have their limitations. This is possibly best highlighted in relation to Susan's situation, described earlier.

As you will recall, Susan was a 23-year-old single carer who was living in run-down accommodation with few supports to help her with the care of her two small children. She was referred to social work services by her health visitor following a suicide attempt. Susan had a number of immediate issues that were causing her concern around finances, housing and child-care arrangements: areas that would all lend themselves to task-centred casework. She also had issues about the setting of limits for her children around bedtimes, where they could play and what they were allowed to do within the house, issues that would lend themselves to using behavioural methods of intervention. Susan also had deep concerns about repeating her own parents' mistakes and was depressed about how this reflected on her own developing mothering skills, underlying issues that might be impacting on her present world and consequently might potentially be remedied using psychosocial casework. She was also isolated, felt stigmatised by her lone parenthood and was generally negative about her future life chances, issues that could lend themselves to group work, particularly from a feminist perspective. In this context, any one of the methods could potentially provide a starting point for working with Susan.

How then are decisions made about method selection in this situation? Given the number of issues with which Susan was confronted, not all could be responded to immediately. With the help of the worker, Susan needed to begin to prioritise these issues in a way that provided for realistic and achievable goals. This is the essence of planned intervention. Whilst there is more than one possible starting point, in Susan's situation, intervention began by looking at a method that would enable her quickly to build up her confidence and self-esteem, thereby enabling her to feel stronger and reduce some of the many practical difficulties in her life. This was carried out using task-centred casework to work on the debt and safety issues, supported by using a behavioural method with the children to set them a routine and structure, thereby taking some of the pressure off Susan around the continual demands made of her. In this instance, the worker was using two complementary short-term methods to facilitate change. The worker's and Susan's assessment of the situation was that there needed to be a qualitative improvement in her practical situation before she could find the 'emotional space' to move on to other issues. As the situation developed, the worker was able to support and empower Susan to challenge how she felt about her life, using group work and psychosocial casework. This is an example of a strategic, planned response to using methods, which requires good assessment and organisational skills. Utilising methods of intervention involves listening carefully to the needs articulated by the service user and responding to his/her priorities for change. In this situation, practical needs were to the fore; in another situation it might have been more deep-seated psychological needs. Every situation requires to be assessed on its merits (see Table 7.1).

What Susan's situation highlights is that even the simplest of plans require workers to identify some process of intervention that they and the service users ideally attempt to follow (Tossell and Webb 1986). This provides a baseline, purpose and rationale for action. Methods of intervention, however, need not be utilised on their own. As Susan's situation illustrates, it is possible to use more than one method at a time. Each method has perceived strengths and limitations and workers may use them in a complementary manner to respond in a planned and structured way. Whilst workers may favour one method, it is important that method selection should not become routinised or proceduralised but remain a conscious process of choice on each occasion – *selection* is the key. The challenge for the professional worker working from an empowering and anti-oppressive perspective is to ensure that the intervention focuses clearly on the needs of the service user rather than solely on the exigencies of the service. This means that workers need to select carefully from a range of potential methods of intervention the one which is most appropriate to the situation. Tempting though it may be to operate 'the way we

Table 7.1 Methods potentially available

Presenting problem	Potential method of intervention	Process and likely outcome
Financial Issues Housing Child-care	Task-centred	By careful exploration of the issues and negotiation around the tasks to be undertaken, Susan could be encouraged to take control of her situation and develop her own strategies and solutions.
Setting limits on children's behaviour	Behavioural	Susan would be encouraged to focus on the behaviour patterns and to develop responses to the children which would help her develop a sense of control and confidence over her parenting. By separating the behaviour from the person, Susan would be likely to avoid any further deterioration in her relationship with her children.
Concerns about her parenting capacity	Psychosocial	By setting aside time in a safe environment, Susan could begin to reflect on the nature and quality of her own experience of being parented. This would allow her to integrate the positive and negative aspects of the process.

do it here', this is not empowering nor could it be considered to be ethical or inclusive practice. Professional social work practice, regardless of the setting, takes place within a milieu that needs to be acknowledged when developing an intervention strategy. Workers do not function independently of the social and political context, nor are they free to make unrestricted decisions. Therefore, an understanding of these competing demands and the worker's ability to influence decision-making processes will impact on method selection. While this is by no means an exhaustive list, factors that are likely to influence the process of selecting a method of intervention will include:

● the assessment of the situation

● the agency context

- the worker's approach and skills

- the service user's abilities and supports.

These factors are not mutually exclusive, nor do they appear in any hier-archical order. They do however form the baseline from which to develop planned intervention.

Assessment of the Situation

The starting point for selecting a method is assessment, which should produce as full and accurate a picture of the service user and the situation as possible. Gathering information to formulate assessments is part of the ongoing process of work with service users. As Coulshed and Orme (1998, p. 21) rightly identify, 'assessment is an ongoing process'. The focus, however, changes as the purpose of the assessment moves towards intervention on a planned basis. In order to select an appropriate method of intervention, assessment must be focused and purposeful. The worker needs to be clear about the scope of the 'problem' and the methods of intervention that can potentially bring about its resolution. Ethical and effective practice demands that this be informed by the 'voice' of the service user whilst acknowledging the primary purpose for which the working relationship was created.

Whilst the reality of much modern social work is that resources, and in particular the worker's time, are often rationed, this should not mean that the service given should be diluted. Rationing, should it occur, is about who receives the service in the first place, not the nature of that service or the methods of intervention utilised to provide it. Methods, to be effective, cannot be partially implemented. If, for example, a contract established using a task-centred method requires eight sessions, an effec-tive outcome will not be achieved by arbitrarily reducing this to five simply on the basis of pressures of staff time. Failure appropriately to apportion resources may lead to dilution and, consequently, poor-quality provision that fails to achieve results, far less those desired by the worker and the service user. This is a situation that is not conducive to either a managerial or professional agenda on good practice.

Assuming that we are able to resource our intervention, it is vital to keep the service user at the heart of the process of method selection. In some situations, this will include deciding who actually *is* the service user. It is not always apparent who it is that needs to engage with the worker to effect change. Assumptions may be made based on gender or racial stereo-types. For example, within the context of community care, assumptions are often made about the role of women as carers, leading workers to concentrate their efforts on those whom they perceive as being the potential targets for change (Dalley 1996; Orme 2001). Deciding who should be the focus of the work is clearly a matter of judgement about the factors that have caused the situation, the depth of the problem and how this is perceived by both the service user and others. Adopting an uncritical approach to 'who is the service user?' can lead to oppressive practice. As part of the engagement and assessment process, the worker needs to negotiate with the service user to reach an understanding of the issue(s) to be addressed and consequently the method(s) employed. Such discussions need to take account not only of the nature of the problem but also the urgency and the consequences of *not* intervening (Doel and Marsh 1992). This requires active listening on the part of the worker, who needs to be able to assess a situation where the tasks identified as being the most important have to wait until an urgent issue has been attended to. For example, in the early stages of working with Susan, it was clear that in her view what she needed to work on was her debts. Whilst these had persisted for some time and therefore could have been considered non-urgent, she was unable to move on to deal with other more fundamental issues such as child-care or her health until these had been addressed. Whilst they were not the most important issues, they had an urgency for Susan and consequently the potential to jeopardise the success of any future intervention if not addressed. The implications of this were that the methods initially employed were short-term as a response to perceived urgent need, while the more intractable issues responded better to longer-term methods such as group work. What is important when looking at methods of intervention is that where the process of assessment is shared with and understood by the service user, its chances of success will arguably increase.

Agency Context

Workers rarely practise independently (Alaszewski and Manthorpe 1990); instead they are employed by agencies that are organised to provide services for particular purposes, within the overall statutory context, which will have implications for the planning process employed with service users (Braye and Preston–Shoot 1995). The growing diversity of organisations and agencies that employ social workers, including those in the voluntary and private sectors, means that it is increasingly problematic to make generalisations about which agencies utilise which method. This fragmentation of traditional practices related to specific agencies has been compounded by the breaking-down of the 'fault line' between areas such as health and social work in recent years, particularly at the practice level (Challis et al. 2002). Whilst joint working between agencies and sectors has led to new opportunities and challenges for practice, it has also had implications for professional and agency autonomy. For example, Webb and Levin (2000), in their study of community care services, found that whilst most social workers were welcoming of the reforms, many also felt that their practice had become more superficial, reactive and geared towards assessment rather than planned intervention. This notion of inter-agency work impacting on worker and agency autonomy and potentially leading to compromises in service delivery for service users as agencies sought common ground was also found by Challis et al. (2002). What these studies highlight is that agency/interagency context undoubtedly impacts on workers' abilities to shape intervention.

The impact of agency on method selection is probably most apparent when we look at the growing managerial culture impacting on all sectors of service delivery, including the voluntary sector (Clarke and Newman 1997). Whilst there is a wide range of organisational structures, the growth in managerialism has meant they are increasingly organised on bureaucratic principles, based on top-down lines of communication and decision-making with hierarchical control structures. Consequently, the workers' roles in these settings are often prescribed. In this context, methods that stress clear resource-awareness around 'what works' have tended to come to the fore, stimulating a move towards short-term, time-limited methods which can arguably be economically justified (Howe 1996). This is particularly true of criminal justice, which has been at the forefront of developing evidence-based methods such as the cognitive behavioural method (Raynor 1996), but is also increasingly the case across all of the sectors serving social work. What the above factors suggest is that the worker's ability to practise will be limited, often within predetermined parameters influenced by state legislation and the policy and procedures of the agency. Whilst acknowledging that agencies can influence the utilisation of methods, restricting service to short-term, evidenced-based work, this may in itself be problematic. Of concern within this culture is the danger that if service users are given a service that does not meet their needs, they are liable to return to the agency looking for further assistance to deal with their situations.

Whilst organisational policies and procedures are important in terms of method selection, as Thompson (2000) points out, the culture of the work setting is also important. Thompson (2000, p. 43–4) succinctly describes the nature and importance of that culture when he says that this 'refers to the set of common patterns, assumptions, values and norms that become established within an organization over a period of time. It is summed up in the phrase: "the way we do things around here".' Therefore, we need to understand not only what the organisation claims it wants to occur, but

also what happens in reality, as this is filtered through the eth
organisation. Workplace culture can impact on the meth
For example, a concern for many students and new workers is that the
workplace cultures are based on a competitive atmosphere where ability is
assessed according to the machismo of the number of cases managed
rather than the quality of what is provided to service users. This may have
negative effects on the worker through pressure to perform and may mean
that there is a push towards using less time-consuming methods. It can
also mean a rejection of the most appropriate method of intervention. In
large hierarchical organisations, such as local authority social services and
many voluntary organisations, this distinction between intention and
reality is of considerable importance. It is what enables local practice to
develop and, in particular, influences what workers believe is expected of
them by the agency.

Arguably, local practices are among the main factors restricting the use
of planned intervention – methods – in the workplace, as workers follow
accepted custom and practice rather than looking to what would be the
most appropriate method(s) for this service user. Therefore, when starting
to consider selecting a method, there are both organisational pressures
and personal/service user complexities that will influence the ability to
act. This is why social work is more than just a 'doing' process; it should
also be an effective and ethical activity as individual workers develop a
professional not just a bureaucratic response to the pressures they face.
In this context, we agree with Thompson (2000, p. 81), who states that 'an
accountable professional is one who takes responsibility for whatever is
reasonably possible to pursue professional aims and this includes making
a positive contribution towards influencing the organisation in order to
maximise the potential for achieving those aims'. What he is highlighting
is that professional practice implies more than acceptance of any situation, but instead involves workers utilising their skills, knowledge and
abilities to meet the service users' needs. Professionals are not there merely
to follow instructions, but to look beyond what is demanded of them
by the organisation and to develop practice to provide the best service. In
terms of selecting a method, this will involve more than just fitting the
service user to the worker's or the agency's favoured way of working, but
looking at what is best for the service user and finding ways of making this
happen.

The Worker's Approach

Payne (1997) suggests that the relationship between workers and service
users is an interactive one, with both being able to learn from each other.

It involves a two-way process, with the influence of workers being challenged and changed by service users. From the perspective of the individual worker, this can be both positive and negative in terms of the learning process, as the worker is able to learn what works, what is realistic and what is achievable in a range of settings. However, it also implies the potentially more painful experience of learning what does not work and having to reflect upon one's own limitations in that context. Part of this learning process is the need to be aware not only of our *value base*, but also of what knowledge and skills we bring to the situation. If, for example, the worker's approach is procedural, the involvement of the service user in the selection of a method of intervention may be marginal, as the process is likely to be driven by the organisational concerns of the service agency. Self-determination and democratic empowerment may not be values that the worker considers as central to the service provided and this will eventually impact on the methods selected.

Appropriate *knowledge* of, for example, sociological and psychological theories will help the worker understand the service user in the situation, although the application of such theories to the actual living reality of the service user can be problematic (Howe 1987; Payne 1997). Knowledge of relevant current research can also help inform the worker about the appropriateness of particular methods within a specific context (Trevithick 2000). Equally, a clear understanding of the legal mandate for action is important as a means of informing method selection. Even with this knowledge base in place, workers may not have the capacity to apply the method in practice owing to the lack of *skills*. Interestingly, in our experience as social work educators, most students relate this lack of skills to psychosocial methods as opposed to others. Whilst they feel they understand the theory of this method, there is less certainty around having the skills, support and understanding to put it into practice. This tends to occur because they feel that psychosocial casework deals with underlying problems that are more difficult to work on than the practical activities all too often associated with surface methods of intervention. This may be a false assumption in that to be able to use any of the methods is a complex and skilled activity that takes time and practice to perfect. It is not enough to know about a method of intervention; workers also require the skills to put it into practice. This means that workers need a range of skills to enable the methods to work (Thompson 2000; Trevithick 2000). Whilst this list is not exhaustive, key skills in this area are communication, emotional literacy, empathy, listening, planning, time management and – in particular – good negotiating skills.

Workers are unlikely to have the full range of potential methods of intervention available to them and even the most established practitioners experience a skills gap from time to time. What is important is not to present an image to the service user of the worker as the 'expert' who will resolve the situation but rather of the worker who will often have to develop skills whilst working directly with the service user. This requires a degree of honesty on the part of the worker around what is achievable within their range of capabilities. While this may be slightly uncomfortable for workers, service users are likely to be reassured if they are able to respond openly and honestly (NISW 1996, p. 7). Fundamental to making this process of learning in practice work is that all workers require good support and supervision. This supportive environment is required to enable the worker to reflect upon the assumptions being made about service users and their capabilities, particularly in relation to gender, race, age or disability. What is crucial in relation to reflection is that workers do not allow internalised bias to get in the way of what the service user requires to work on to change the situation.

Being able to appreciate the situation from the service user's perspective is an important aspect of an anti-discriminatory approach and will assist the worker, in partnership and discussion with the service user, to select the most appropriate method to fit the situation. Of particular concern, in this context, is that many service users, as Trevithick (2000, p. 2) suggests, lead complicated and chaotic lives, which means that workers make assumptions about service users' lives and what is required to support them to create structure and organisation. Therefore, when we are considering methods in relation to service users, it is crucial to see them as unique individuals, rather than adopting stereotypical responses. This can be particularly important if the worker is in a setting where the range of people using the service is limited. It is crucial not to see the service user as a 'single carer', 'prisoner', 'rebellious adolescent', etc. Working within an anti-oppressive framework, it is vital that workers explore directly with service users how they see the situation and what possible outcomes they may wish to secure.

It is also important to bear in mind the capabilities and skills that the service user brings to the process of change when selecting and implementing methods of intervention. Given that much of the contact that workers have with service users derives from problematic situations, it is tempting to adopt a deficit view of service users. If workers aspire to practise in an empowering way, it is crucial that work be undertaken from a perspective which values and builds upon strengths. Equally, however, the assessment of skills must be realistic so that service users are not subjected to a process that reinforces their need for assistance. Good practice does, however, require workers to listen carefully to how the service user articulates the pressures they perceive themselves to face, rather than making assumptions (NISW 1996).

This active listening and sharing of perspectives may not always feature in the process of method selection. There would seem to be two reasons for this lack of consulting, informing and listening to those using the service about how workers intend to work alongside them in their lives. First, most methods are designed from the worker's perspective rather than that of the service user. Secondly, workers often assume that the methods are too complex and therefore cannot be understood by service users who are struggling to make sense of their current situations. In relation to service users' understanding how the methods of intervention work, the emphasis in this situation has to be on the worker being able succinctly to explain the aims and purpose in a manner and in language that service users can understand. Explaining the intention and under-pinning assumptions regarding the workers' intervention undoubtedly raises questions about service users' willingness to engage with the process. As Trotter (1999) rightly points out, not all social work service users have a choice about their involvement. Susan, for example, had little say in whether she accepted the service, owing to the potential for statutory intervention around the care of her children. In the early days of her involvement, her view of the task-centred programme that was drawn up was strongly influenced by the threat she perceived of losing her children. She accepted the social worker's presence, but went through the motions rather than actively participating. At a more general level, as Mayer and Timms (1970) suggested over thirty years ago, service users do not like methods that are vague and focus on insight. If workers are approaching the process of method selection in a genuinely empowering way, they need to ensure that they are actively listening to the service users' percep-tion of the change required. It is difficult, for example, to work within the structured framework of task-centred work when the service user's lifestyle is chaotic and unstructured. While they may agree to the suggested method, this may lead to unrealistic goal-setting if the worker is not prop-erly attuned to the service user's situation. As Taylor and Devine (1993, p. 4) state, 'the client's perception of the situation has to be the basis for effective social work'. If we do not start from where the client is, how can we expect them to engage with us?

The Service User's Strengths and Resources

Whilst the worker is important in relation to selecting a method, so too is the service user's situation and capabilities. As Howe (1987, p. 3) states, 'the client's perception is an integral part of the practice of social work'. To ensure that this perception has validity, workers will need to involve and inform service users from the outset about their concerns, responsibilities and ability to negotiate solutions. This is not as easy an activity as some might imagine, as workers need to have a deep understanding of their own situation, professionally and in a wider work context (Jordan 2004). Negotiation requires skill and confidence on the part of workers as they attempt to secure for the service user an appropriate package of services from the 'managerial elite' (Lymbery 2001, p. 378). As social workers increasingly find themselves working within secondary settings or complex interdisciplinary teams, the ability to articulate clearly the needs of service users from a social work perspective becomes more difficult.

In a study carried out with a range of community care workers in Gateshead, they indicated that they felt the need to compromise on some aspects of the professional role in order to reach an acceptable working partnership (Challis 2002). In addition, some service users may not welcome this, owing to issues around their own self-esteem or reluctance to accept social work support. They often have their own set of assumptions about what social work is and what workers are able to provide, based on past experiences and relationships. This is particularly true of black service users whose experience of social work may reflect a service that has in the past been inappropriate for their needs (Milner and O'Byrne 1998, p. 23). This should not discourage working in an open and honest manner, but should increase awareness that it often takes time to empower people and enable them to raise their sense of self-worth. Failure to start from this point may mean that the service user is being fitted to the service rather than the other way round.

Methods should be built upon the strengths as well as the limitations of the service user. We should look to improving service users' lives, not just highlighting their difficulties and limitations. Crucially, workers need to be aware that social work itself and social work training tend to be based on a deficit model, which limits the ability to consider the complexity of service users' strengths in social situations. Traditionally, methods have looked for the difficulties in the service user's life and what could be done to remedy this shortfall (Milner 2001). The difficulty with this starting point, as Fook (2002) points out, is that if people are asked about their problems, then that is what is heard and will be the basis of the worker's relationship with them. Whilst it is impossible to ignore that service users are looking for a service because of what are often negative situations, they also have strengths and skills that need to be encouraged and drawn upon in the social work relationship. Relating this to Susan, she had until fairly recently been able to balance the many responsibilities of lone parenthood, demonstrating perseverance and commitment to her children in difficult circumstances. Therefore, working with her initially using a task-centred method valued the positives she could bring to the situation, enabling her to take action to progress her situation. However, as we noted earlier, Susan had underlying reasons for her actions that also needed to be challenged. In this respect, the task-centred method was used to tackle those issues that were stopping the longer-term work, to build up Susan's confidence and to establish the relationship positively for future psychosocial casework.

The level of support that service users have will also influence the method or range of methods chosen. This can take the form of friends or relatives or other agencies in the community. The danger for busy workers is that they can overlook this area and consequently place all the time and energy of the method process on the service user – somebody who may already be at breaking-point in terms of the demands their world creates. Susan provides an example of this point in practice. She was highly motivated to change her life, but had limited support networks in her local area, which meant that her child-care arrangements provided real limitations to undertaking intensive methods of intervention such as task-centred or behavioural methods. Any plan of action needed to respect the fact that her situation was both disorganised and fraught with the demands and needs of having sole care of two small children. Had she had a wider range of supports, then they could have taken some responsibility for the children, enabling Susan to take more control over her life sooner. The choice for social workers is they can either build in supports so that the work can be undertaken more quickly or they may need to be more flexible and adapt the methods. In relation to Susan's situation, the solution was to build in a befriender/support worker in order that she could have time out from her children for social activities and to work on the identified issues she wanted to resolve. This is not to say that alternatives will always be possible or that family and friends are able to provide positive support, but this should be an area that is considered when we look at the ability of service users to utilise methods.

It is also important to be clear about the target of any intervention process. Much social work intervention takes place with women, not necessarily because the 'problems' are theirs but because they are the ones who are willing to engage with the process. If we examine the issue of poverty, for example, Glendinning and Millar (1992) suggest that family income is not evenly distributed between the men and women sharing a household: women are more likely to spend on routine, day-to-day expenses such as food, clothing, heating, etc., while men are more inclined to spend on luxury items or goods for their own use; budgetary power within the household, therefore, tends to remain with the men. When workers become involved with families where household budgeting is an issue, there is a tendency to limit the dialogue to the female service user, who may not be the one who is responsible for the financial difficulties (Hill and Laing 1995). In any process of intervention, therefore, it is important to target those who need to change rather than those who are more receptive to social work intervention.

Many service users come to the social work relationship with low confidence or looking for answers or have become used to workers assuming the role of expert, factors that have been learned from their life experience or previous work with social work agencies. This can militate against a more open relationship and compromise the worker into assuming the powerful role of making decisions that could be shared with the service user. Whilst there are no easy answers to this situation, what it does highlight is that working in partnership does not detract from workers having to make decisions. At times, the decision may be to take control until the service user has built up more confidence or skills. This reflects the fact that service-user involvement is often a process to be worked towards rather than an instant reality achieved through desire alone. What is important is that these decisions should be transparent to the service user, as far as possible, and that when assuming responsibility the worker should be developing the starting point of the relationship, which should have as its ultimate goal service users taking control over their own lives.

Skills for Method Selection – Decision-making in Practice

One of the key elements of method selection is decision-making, ranging from those at a microlevel to those bigger decisions that determine the opportunities and actions of service users (DHSS 1985; Pratt 2000). It is an activity that requires constant vigilance and reflection on the part of the worker to ensure that the most effective decisions are made. The process of decision-making in terms of selecting a method has tended either to be seen as 'obvious', flowing automatically from the gathering of data and therefore not requiring thought, or based on intuitive experience. The outcome of these forms of decision-making often reflect the worker's preferred option rather than the service user's needs and abilities. However, whether they are consciously thought through or part of a repertoire of responses, the decisions made have real implications for the service user. Consequently, workers need to move beyond intuition constantly to reflect upon and evaluate the decisions and consequent choices that they make. Unless this key skill is understood and developed by workers, then they may unwittingly reinforce many of the existing power relationships to the detriment of the service user (Jordan 2004). A procedural approach to practice, for example, may lead workers to believe that the scope for making decisions rests primarily with them, that they have the expertise to decide what is in the best interests of the service user. This may be because their view of the overall situation suggests that, in terms of selecting which method to utilise, the options available are limited and that they as workers are best placed to make the choices. In some situations, the possibility that alternative methods of intervention are available may not even be considered as the practice of the agency favours one particular method. It is, therefore, important that workers make clear and conscious decisions around their choice of method of intervention.

Recent years have seen a growth in frameworks that have been designed to enable workers to structure their thoughts and responses in relation to decision-making, none more so than in the field of risk analysis (Parton 1996; Pratt 2000). Whilst these frameworks are still relatively crude and do not provide the complete answer, they enable workers to consider the range of possible options and the consequences of the choices that are made, making them more open and accountable for both the service user and the worker in relation to their agency. As Thompson (2002, pp. 206–7) puts it, 'the challenge of decision-making, then is that of looking at options, evaluating which we feel is the most appropriate way forward and then watching carefully to see whether we have made the right move'. This is an activity that requires workers to be informed, aware of their biases and limitations and able to reflect on and evaluate their decisions.

When reflecting on decision-making in relation to selecting a method, what becomes apparent is the importance of involving the service user at every stage and being clear about who has the power to make what decisions. Providing a clear but brief account of the available methods and their relative strengths and limitations to the service user enables a process of informed negotiation around those which seem most appropriate to the service user's current situation. It should not be assumed that this can be completely unfettered but rather that it is informed by the practical realities of the situation in terms of the perhaps conflicting perspectives of agency, worker and service user. By being open and honest, workers will have a much greater chance of being effective as they will be working with the most appropriate information about the situation and crucially will have the investment of service users in the process. However, even the best thought-out and best-planned decisions cannot guarantee success, as social work practice is about dealing with uncertainty, in relation to both the information gathered and people's capabilities. Ethical and effective practice requires that workers constantly review their chosen way of working in terms of its appropriateness for service users and the situation.

The complexity of the service users' situation creates the potential for a range of competing solutions. Whilst decision-making frameworks imply a logical process that should be followed, working with real service users may impact on the ability sequentially to follow such a process. No matter what methods are used, workers will always need to exercise their own judgement in relation to the process, what information is obtained and the choices that have to be made. This complexity and uncertainty is part of the professional task, but workers should ensure that they are supported in this activity both formally and informally. Drawing upon supervision, research about what works and current understanding of best practice can provide safeguards for both the service user and the worker. Working in this informed manner should provide the basis for an empowering practice that is open, structured and planned. What it will not provide is a blueprint for action with all service users in similar situations. This is a fundamental component of social work practice and reinforces the notion that it is not an activity the lends itself to formulaic responses. Part of the artistry of social work practice is the subtle combination of intellectual rigour and the more intangible aspects of flair and creativity. This makes selecting a method of intervention a complex process but one that, if it is truly empowering and inclusive, can lead to lasting and effective change.

Summary of Chapter

1. Selecting a method is rarely a straightforward activity, but is instead influenced by a variety of factors, including the assessment of the situation, the worker's approach, skills and abilities, the service user's strengths and capabilities and agency context.

2. No individual worker can be expected to understand and apply the full range of social work methods. What is important is that workers understand their own skills and abilities in relation to methods and look to develop these over time, including the ability to select across the range of methods in order that they can meet the service users' needs and concerns. In this context it is crucial that full consideration be given to what service users can positively bring to the situation, as well as the more traditional concerns about their limitations.

3. Workers rarely practise independently of the legal and organisational context of the state or large organisation that delivers services. This is a situation that places limitations on their professional autonomy and is often further restricted by the workplace culture and its impact on practice. However, working professionally in an empowering manner means that, whilst acknowledging these parameters, workers have to continue to assert what is the best possible service and advocate that this be provided in the most appropriate manner.

4. Selecting a method is a process that involves both the worker and the service user making decisions about what is the most appropriate way to progress the situation. Unless this key skill is understood and

put into practice, workers may unconsciously reinforce many of the existing power relationships to the detriment of the service user. In recent years there has been a growing move towards developing frameworks for decision-making. Whilst helpful in drawing out our thought processes for discussion, these frameworks do not take away from the fact that selecting a method is a subjective process influenced by the worker's and service user's knowledge, skills and values.

8

Reflection and Supervision

The content of this text so far has focused on the nature and process of social work intervention and the role of the worker therein. This chapter begins to explore the means by which workers develop their abilities to reflect upon their intervention within a structured environment. It is important for workers to be able to take a step back from their practice and begin to identify any patterns that may emerge, lessons that can be learned, adjustments that need to be made. In this way, past experiences, formal knowledge and learning, including policies and procedure, are critically built upon to develop present and future practice. This learning from experience is the aim of reflective practice, as workers openly and honestly re-evaluate their work. As has been examined elsewhere in this text, the workers' approach to practice will inform and shape their understanding of the situation, which in turn will shape their reflection in relation to how they *name* and *frame* the problem (Schön 1987).

The debate about the role and future of social work is also reflected in the professional education of workers, where a tension exists between the notions of education and training and how best to equip new workers for the demands of a constantly evolving role. Training fits more closely with the managerial agenda and its emphasis on technical skills and task completion; education relates to the professional agenda of developing understanding and learning. That said, what students learn and how they learn continues to be the focus of discussion and research (Marsh and Triseliotis 1996; Lyons and Manion 2004). Whilst this debate is unlikely to have any clear resolution, what is important is that it takes place free of rigid stances and uncritical thinking. It is in this context of critical thinking that reflection obtains prominence, as workers (and agencies) need constantly to review their experiences to ensure that they are providing the best possible service in the most effective and ethical manner. However, whilst learning from practice using reflection is the professional responsibility of all workers, it is not a solitary activity and needs to be located in an agency context. This provides the supports and enables practitioners not just to meet the needs of the organisation but also to

127

develop their own knowledge and skills. The aim of this and the next chapter is to explore how we can use reflection, supervision and evaluation to enhance practice for workers, service users and agencies.

What Do We Mean by Reflection?

The concept of the 'reflective practitioner' now pervades most professional groupings, and social work is no exception. However, it is not a new concept. Dewey (1933), an educationalist writing over seventy years ago, first defined 'reflective practice' as learning which is built over time as we experience new situations and processes. What he identified was that it was not the nature of the *experience* that was important but the nature of the *learning* obtained from it that mattered. The message from Dewey's work was that both positive and negative experiences provide opportunities for workers to learn, and what is important is that they critically and constructively use these to enhance practice. In recent years reflective practice has gained increasing prominence in the professional agenda, particularly the work of Schön (1983), who relates its importance to developing understanding and practice in the uncertain and complex world of service users. For Schön (1983), this learning needs to take place at the level of not just cognition but also awareness, feelings and intuition. Despite this long tradition, reflection is a contested concept, with some viewing it as an essential defining feature of modern professionalism (Schön 1987) while others would claim that it is much more difficult to define and apply in practice (Ixer 1999). Ixer argues that refection raises more questions than it answers, as it is at best a vague concept with no proven link to developing practice. Whilst accepting its subjectivity and limited research base, reflection is more than just evidencing outcomes, important as this may be for good practice. It is also about exploring our theorising, skills and feelings with the intention of learning from experience in order that we can improve future provision. As Eby (2000, p. 52) suggests, 'reflection enables individuals to make sense of their lived experiences through examining such experiences in context'. What is apparent in this definition is that reflection, whilst subjective, is a structured and organised activity that is dependent upon workers reviewing and evaluating their formal knowledge, past experiences and present feelings and actions in order to examine what has happened and why. The aim of this activity is to change or enhance present or future practice for the benefit of service users.

In reviewing the literature on reflection, what becomes apparent is that it is an activity that workers cannot be expected to be able to undertake without developing their self-awareness and valuing different types of knowledge beyond formal theories, including practice knowledge developed by workers in action (Fook 2002). Reflective practice in this respect is a proactive activity that asks workers to take responsibility for their learning and for developing solutions to service users' situations, rather than looking to fixed responses or procedures for answers. What it does not provide, however, is the certainty that many workers and approaches seek to obtain, although we would argue that it is a skill that can be developed over time (Schön 1991). Our experience of students developing reflective skills is that at first, particularly in initial practice placements, they tend to *reflect on action*. It is after the event that they are able to make the connection between theory, skills and values and their practice. Whilst this is a legitimate starting point for workers using their experience to learn, it does have the disadvantage that it can only benefit existing service users retrospectively. As they progress through their education, however, students move on to *reflection in action* as they make the connections between taught theory, experience and feelings whilst working with the service user. This move from reflection *on* to *in* action is often the result of hard work, pain and soul-searching on the students' part as they seek to examine their contribution to the social work process (Fisher and Somerton 2000). What is difficult about this process for workers is the need to be open and honest with themselves about what they have done and why, answering questions about the effectiveness of their intervention. Therefore, despite its acceptance of subjectivity, reflective practice does not imply eschewing evaluation or rigour; it is at the core of this form of practice.

One of the issues with reflection is that because it is about developing our learning from experience, each reflective episode will have its own unique aspects that are dependent upon a variety of factors, including who the worker is and what he or she wants to consider, be it a specific aspect of practice or their overall intervention (Quinn 2000). The information gleaned from this process may relate only to a particular situation. However, this should not stop us from being rigorous and organised in how we undertake this task. For example, Gibbs (1988) describes the activity of reflection as a cyclical process of learning, where workers builds up their understanding over time. In this respect Figure 8.1 is offered as an aid for structuring reflection.

By portraying reflection as a cycle (Gibbs 1988), it becomes evident that learning is ongoing and evolves through changes in understanding, knowledge, skills and ultimately values, providing insight into how the worker's awareness has changed (*I realise that*); analysing what decisions were made and why (*I decided because*); considering what happened (*I wonder why*) and developing new understanding (*I now think*). Utilising such a framework should enable workers to take stock of their encounters with service users and to create a reference point for future interventions.

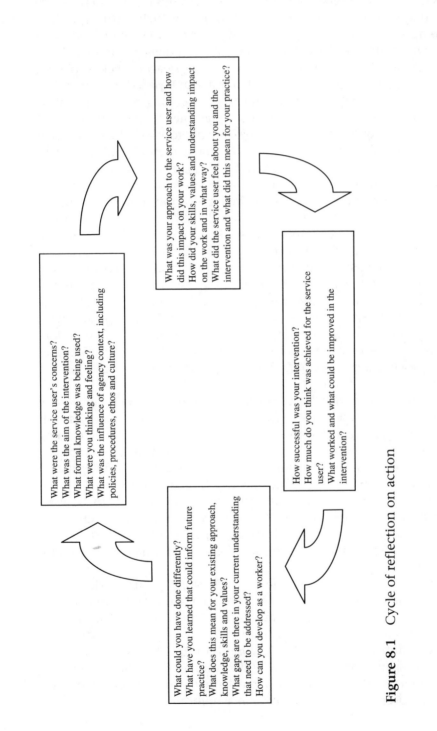

Figure 8.1 Cycle of reflection on action

Working from an empowering perspective, this process also needs workers to take account of the service users' feelings, experiences and opinions, establishing what they understand of the processes involved and how service delivery can be improved. What this process highlights is that reflection is more than a 'commonsense' approach to learning that draws on what we know. Instead it is a more thoughtful and challenging process, which utilises formal knowledge and experience but should also enable workers to generate their own theories for practice. In this respect reflection is not about rejecting formal theory, but about providing a process that gives it real meaning in practice, related to experience, self-awareness and understanding. Theory-building consequently becomes a concrete rather than an abstract activity, distant from practice. Reflection should then enable workers to develop their own theories for practice, which can be used in conjunction with and to compliment formal knowledge.

Building on the reflective process, Quinn (2000, p. 81) identifies the following skills as important in undertaking this activity:

- *retrospection* – thinking back over past events

- *self-evaluation* – critical analysis and evaluation of actions and feelings

- *Reorientation* – influencing the future approach.

Retrospection involves thinking back over past events in an attempt to identify issues, knowledge (formal and experiential) or behaviours that were significant. This can be a difficult process for workers, who may have a tendency to 'do' rather than consciously 'think about' their actions. By going back over the exact sequence of events, it is often possible to identify aspects of the encounter that were not so evident at the time. When this process takes place within the context of supervision, it is important that it does not become a 'blaming' process but retains an openness, which facilitates learning. *Self-evaluation* is a process of re-engaging with the events at a much more conscious level, thinking through the impact and significance of particular aspects of the encounter. It enables workers critically to evaluate actions or feelings in order to understand the reasons why these occurred as they did. They are encouraged to undertake this task as a means of identifying the component parts of any interaction in order that any necessary readjustments can be made. Workers can also utilise this process to re-engage with their own thinking about the situation, which may have been lost in the context of necessary actions. *Reorientation* enables workers to utilise what they have learned from the earlier phases to influence future actions. In the light of greater understanding of the processes at work in any situation, workers may conclude, for example, that a different approach is required, that they could have been more inclusive in their decision-making, that they need to gain more knowledge about a particular issue. Reflection, therefore, for many workers is a retrospective activity (reflection on action) that facilitates the creation of a depth of knowledge and understanding about the process of work undertaken. It enables workers to reaffirm their knowledge and skills and helps to create a very conscious and deliberate approach to practice.

Learning from Experience

The concept of experiential learning is particularly applicable to practice, as it enables us to make sense of the complex range of interactions that occur within any practice situation.

For example, Jane, a 28-year-old single, white female worker was allocated the task of working with Tarjinder and his mother to discuss Ravinder's concerns that his behaviour was becoming difficult to manage. Prior to qualification, Jane had worked for two years as a residential child-care worker, and more recently had spent 18 months in a busy inner-city social services team. As a result of her experiences, Jane considered herself particularly skilled in establishing relationships with young people. Consequently, she entered the initial meeting with the family with a degree of confidence in her ability to assist. During the course of the meeting, however, the discussion became rather heated, with the mother and son talking over each other and not listening to the other's point of view. As the voices grew louder, Jane decided to ask Tarjinder to leave the room for a brief 'time out' to let tempers cool. This was a technique that she had used many times as a residential worker to defuse difficult situations. On this occasion, however, Ravinder became very angry at what she considered to be Jane's undermining of her role as a parent. What did Jane learn from this on reflecting on the situation?

Personal insight. Jane concluded that she found it difficult not to be in control of situations and was much more comfortable working with young people than with adults. She was a bit bewildered by Ravinder's reaction to her attempts to resolve the situation. On reflection, she was aware that her expectations of Ravinder and her son were based on a stereotypical understanding of 'family'. This took no account of the cultural issues that impacted on this mother's ability to meet the needs of her child within a society that was fundamentally racist.

Situational information. Jane's understanding of this meeting was that there was an expectation that she would provide a solution to the family difficulties. Based on her past experience, Jane's approach to practice was a procedural one where she saw herself as having the responsibility of resolving the issues for the family. Jane assumed that Tarjinder had been brought to the social work office with a clear expectation on the part of his mother that some solution would be offered. This was linked to her understanding of the functions of the agency in which she worked and the expectations that she had absorbed from the culture of that organisation, i.e. 'fixing' (Howe 1987).

Future responses. Based on this experience, Jane decided that in future she would clarify expectations at the beginning of any conversation. She also recognised her own need to be in control and decided that she needed to explore this further. She also resolved to find out more about working with families from different cultural backgrounds and using different approaches. She planned to take these issues into her next supervision session.

What Jane was doing, in this example, was stepping back from her work and reflecting upon how processes developed as they did. Could she have done things differently? If so, how and why? To what extent had she attempted to impose her own attitudes and values on to the situation? For example, from an anti-oppressive perspective, Jane became aware of how her actions limited Ravinder's ability to make sense of the interaction between herself and Tarjinder. By sharing their understandings of what had happened, how and why, they were more likely to come to a mutually acceptable evaluation of the situation. By empowering Ravinder in this way, she could begin to value the strengths of her parenting rather than focus on the areas of difficulty. Jane would also gain valuable insight into the social and cultural factors that underpinned Ravinder's parenting style. Although Jane was able to obtain this level of refection by talking to colleagues and taking time to think upon her actions, there are techniques that can be used by the worker to enable this process. Whilst this is not claiming to be a definitive list, useful techniques for refining reflection are critical incident analysis, process recordings, reflective diaries and personal learning audits.

Critical incident analysis is often used in social work practice to assist workers with the development of their critical awareness of the process of work. Within this model, workers are required to ask the question 'Why?' in order that they can begin to look beyond the event itself to the underlying processes (Davies and Kinloch 2000; Fook 2002). By attempting to break down an encounter into its constituent elements, they are able to see more clearly the precise impact of interlocking events. It also provides a potentially more empowering approach to learning, as the emphasis is on workers doing their own learning in a supportive environment.

Fook (2000, p. 10) provides a comprehensive set of questions that can be used critically to analyse the text of any incident. It is helpful to read the full set of questions as provided by Fook but, to provide some indication of the process to be adopted, they can be summarised as follows:

1. What emerging themes and patterns are important to me?

2. Who are the significant people and how do I relate to them?

3. Are all perspectives represented in the narrative?

4. How did I interpret the information available?

5. Could I have done this differently?

6. Is my account based on a particular set of assumptions?

7. Where might such assumptions come from?

8. Are there gaps in my descriptive account?

9. Where do I think power rests in my account of this incident?

By deconstructing the incident in this way, workers begin to draw on a range of aspects of their professional identity. They need to pay close attention to how they construct meaning, their understanding of the service user's situation, their political analysis, and so on. Essentially, they are re-examining their use of self through the filter of their approach to practice.

Process recordings are usually associated primarily with social work training and tend not to be valued by established workers as a means of reviewing practice process and decision-making. As the term suggests, the focus of process recordings is to produce a detailed narrative of a specific encounter in order that it can be unpicked in detail. By revisiting the encounter in such a detailed manner, it is often possible to identify points of difficulty or particular success within the process. Frequently, when discussing an interview with a worker, he or she will describe the process as having moved almost instantaneously from a complete lack of engagement by the service user to an effective discussion. It is when the encounter is narrated in detail that the skills employed by the worker to effect this change in attitude can be identified. Similarly, process recordings can be used as an effective debriefing tool in highly charged emotional situations such as child protection.

Ford and Jones (1987, p. 88) describe the process for workers as providing a written account of:

1. what happened chronologically;

2. what they thought was happening and what they did as a result;

3. what they felt at different stages throughout the session.

Process-recording as a technique does not seek critically to evaluate events. It is a means of setting down in writing an essentially descriptive account that can then be used in any subsequent evaluative process. Rather than encouraging analytical skills at the point of writing, this technique encourages the development of self-awareness that can be a step towards critical evaluation of practice.

Reflective diaries, sometimes referred to as reflective logs, are a very effective means of 'learning how to learn', and continue to be used by workers as a source of information to inform and structure ongoing professional supervision (Ghayle and Lillyman 1997). Using a reflective diary can help workers to step back slightly from their practice and note important aspects of their critical thinking. By creating a reflective account of a past event, this encourages workers to focus much more clearly on the 'why' of intervention rather than the 'how'. This can be particularly helpful to workers who find themselves within an organisational culture that is essentially reactive, as they can take time to structure and plan their involvement, taking account of current theory and research.

In some ways, the use of the term 'diary' can be misleading, as it may tempt users of this tool to note down almost every event in chronological order. To be an effective aid to practice, there needs to be a degree of prior selection of those issues and events in a day that warrant further consideration. It may not be helpful, for example, to list all of the tasks undertaken in a day but could be useful to reflect on why a particular day proved to be stressful and eventful. Reflective diaries can help workers see the patterns that may be developing in their responses to situations, thus providing the impetus for change.

Personal learning audits are about asking workers to examine their journey as practitioners, reflecting on what knowledge, skills and abilities they hold and how this impacts on their desired approach. Whilst they have in the main been used by students undertaking their professional training, they are equally applicable to workers in practice. What sits behind this technique is workers exploring the knowledge and skills that are required in order to undertake their present employment. This enables them to explore their strengths and helps develop a realistic level of confidence in their practice abilities (West and Watson 2002). By utilising a proforma developed specifically for this purpose, workers provide information about the skills and knowledge they have gained or developed since taking up the post. This enables them to begin to consolidate their own sense of what they have learned and what they still need to learn in order to achieve their goals. It also helps them to develop a sense of the overall structure of the organisation, understanding what is expected and can be done in the present work environment. Finally, workers are asked to consider a personal learning plan that can help them to develop their skills over time. It therefore creates a tool that enables workers to establish their own learning needs and develop a strategy to meet them. Perhaps most importantly, this audit process enables workers to learn experientially some of the skills they will need to implement in practice with service users, for example negotiation, discussion and the confrontation of difficult issues (West and Watson 2002). What these techniques highlight for workers is the need constantly to reflect and learn from all aspects of experience, including practice, formal education and agency environment. Each worker will find one technique more helpful than another but what is important is that utilising any one of these techniques helps the process of reflecting on practice to have a structured component.

So far we have tended to consider *reflection on action*, where workers look back on their past experiences and use these to learn about and develop their understanding and practice. However, the reality of much practice is based on *reflection in action*, as workers have to make sense of what they are doing at the time and reflect and act on the immediate situation. Whilst many of the issues and processes already described are relevant to reflection in action, it often becomes an intuitive activity that we may not even be conscious of undertaking (Schön 1983). However, this does not mean that it is an activity devoid of learning or experience, only that we have internalised this so that it becomes part of our day-to-day way of thinking and reacting. What is crucial in reflection in action is that it should be a process that is open to critical scrutiny at the point of direct intervention. It should not be seen as some mystical skill which only the gifted worker has acquired and which cannot subsequently be understood or challenged. Dreyfus et al. (1986) suggest that intuition is a process of understanding that, perhaps because of its negative association with the female psyche, tends to be discounted in terms of its importance for the creation of knowledge and understanding. For Dreyfus et al. the process of intuition develops through a number of stages which they claim delineate the development of the professional from the 'novice' stage through to the 'expert' stage; with the final stage suggesting mastery of the skills required. As the level of skill develops, workers will become more able to identity the elements of the situation which provided them with understanding as to the precise nature of the interaction and how best to respond professionally. This is, in our view, part of the artistry of social work practice where information gathered on an intuitive basis is combined with knowledge, skills, values and prior experience to enable workers to arrive at an appropriate response (Ruch 2000). The worker who encountered John in our case study, for example, may have started out with an intuitive response which suggested that there was more to his situation than a request for advocacy. This became the beginning of an assessment as the worker added knowledge about human development, loss and grief, ageing in Western society, etc., to the skills required to gain his trust and enable him to share his difficulties, These, combined with the worker's prior experiences, began in the process of reflection in action, thereby enabling an implementation plan to be jointly developed.

Professional Practice and Supervision

Good practice is a planned and purposeful activity that needs to be constantly evaluated and reflected upon to ensure that it is both effective and ethical in achieving its aims. What individual workers can do and can be supported to achieve will be influenced by both the intra- and inter-agency context of their own and the service users' situation. Therefore, to undertake good practice, workers need the active support and encouragement of the agency in which they work. Reflection, for example, is highly dependent on the support of other team members, particularly supervisors who can bring fresh perspectives and different contexts to the process. Whilst there are numerous ways in which the agency can support good practice, such as flexible policies and procedures, arguably the most direct and important for workers is the supervisory relationship (Kadushin and Harkness 2002). Most workers do not practise independently and increasingly in recent years have found themselves as part of a team managed by a more senior worker, who is expected to provide supervision. It is in this forum that the individual worker mediates and negotiates with the wider agency and its requirements (Thompson 2002).

There is some confusion amongst fieldworkers and residential workers about supervision and its purposes and functions. Even when workers have expectations for something called 'supervision' to be available, there may be little agreement as to what it is or what form it should take. It follows, therefore, that one of the first steps in the development of a supervision scheme is to ensure that those involved come to some understanding of what it entails and what it aims to achieve. Whilst this will have a personal perspective dependent on the worker and agency context, supervision should have the following as its overall aims:

● to improve the quality of service delivered by the worker to service users;

● to support the worker and promote professional development;

● to establish accountability, both of the worker to the organisation and of the organisation to the worker (Kadushin and Harkness 2002).

In some respects 'supervision' is an unfortunate term, as it tends to give the impression that it is only the third aim – accountability – that is important, and even then it is that of the worker to the organisation. This would appear to be the case in the present managerial culture, where supervision is often associated with accountability, giving direction and checking up on the workers' activities (Flynn 1997; Banks 2004). Whilst this is undoubtedly part of the supervisory task, accountability is also a two-way process and should enable workers to have expectations that are met by the organisation. When this fails to materialise, it is little wonder that both workers and supervisors feel uneasy with the process and avoid the activity. Good supervision is more than one-dimensional, it should be for the benefit of all parties, with its primary purpose to develop and benefit the worker and subsequently the service user (Hawkins and Shohet 2000). In this context, accountability takes on a new meaning, enabling workers to know where they stand in relation to the agency, what they can do and how they will be supported in this process. Whilst this should be a negotiated activity, it would be foolish to ignore the obvious power differential that exists in the supervisory relationship. At a simple level, workers hold knowledge and power in relation to their professional position, their understanding of the service users' situation and the demands of their overall workload. The supervisor holds positional power and usually a wider understanding of the managerial culture and ethos of the agency and its subtleties and complexities in practice. It is important that these differences be transparent and acknowledged so that workers and supervisors understand and respond in an environment of honesty and trust. Failure to do this is part of the reason why so much supervision is vague, lacks purpose or slips into checking up on or sharing what is of immediate concern (Hawkins and Shohet 2000).

A common view of supervision is that it is a formal activity, usually on a one-to-one basis, that takes place in the form of regular meetings at a prearranged time and place. Indeed, for many this is the only recognised form of supervision (Thompson 2002). Conversely, not to have 'supervision' usually refers to the absence of regular, formal supervision sessions. With informal supervision, workers often seek support and guidance outside formal meetings to resolve more pressing concerns. However, this does not mean that such conversations are devoid of the accountability of more formal supervision sessions, only that the context may be more informal, not what is discussed or agreed. Whilst regular and formal supervision is important, it is also an informal activity that can take place with not just individuals but also groups (Kadushin and Harkness 2002). Supervision is not always best provided on a one-to-one basis. Atherton (1986), for example, suggests that, in the field of residential care, this traditional model may be limited in that it fails to acknowledge the group-care context of much service delivery and the shared support, guidance and accountability in that context. These factors, if solely dealt with in a one-to-one forum, may lose their relevance to practice. However, despite having much wider possibilities, for many workers 'real' supervision is still perceived as the traditional context, no matter how helpful or unhelpful. In our view, workers and supervisors should consider what is the most appropriate supervision for their setting and should blend the formal and the informal to provide maximum support to workers in complex situations and work environments.

The Elements of Supervision

To achieve the aims of supervision, it must be structured and have purpose. How this is done will be shaped by a number of factors such as work context and personal preference. However, no matter what form it takes, good supervision is a process that should include managing the work-load for both the worker and agency, should be a forum for learning and problem-solving and should be supportive and enabling (Kadushin and Harkness 2002). Whilst in reality these elements often overlap and impact on each other, we want to give some consideration to them individually.

The *managing* element, as we have already seen, is related to issues of accountability, including the monitoring and evaluation of the work. Accountability within this context is likely to be related to the organisation and perhaps the legislative framework, rather than the service user (Preston-Shoot 2001). This element often involves the supervisor in a process of overseeing the day-to-day functioning of the worker in terms of the needs of the organisation. It is also likely to include the allocation of tasks, together with discussion about the progress of particular pieces of work. For most workers, this is a process that is not about their professional development but rather is more closely linked to ensuring that lines of accountability are being appropriately fulfilled. As Thompson (2000) points out, this need not be experienced as a negative activity but can also be a source of reassurance to workers, who know where they stand and that issues will be picked up promptly. In terms of agency accountability to workers, this should also be established in supervision, providing workers with the opportunity to negotiate and mediate, balancing many of the agencies' requirements against the reality of the pressure and demands they face in their daily work. For example an often-neglected activity in this context is workload management, which should be used to ensure that workers have the time and resources to carry out their work properly. What is important to bear in mind is that this element will often openly reflect the power of the organisation over the worker.

The *learning and problem-solving* element should move beyond checking out, to consider how the service is delivered and what workers need to do to improve their ability to provide a quality service. This should be a negotiated and shared activity, looking for solutions that are mutually acceptable to both worker and agency and that best meet the service user's situation. In this respect, supervision should consider problem-solving in relation to individual service users, as well as reflecting on factors such as the worker's approach and service user's needs and how these are impacting on what is being provided. This is where the supervisor is able to utilise a range of strategies to assist the development of critical-thinking skills and provide a safe environment within which the worker can become a more conscious practitioner. The key to this activity will be the quality of the relationship between both parties and the ability to trust and respect difference in that context. This element should also consider the issue of personal development for workers in relation to both their own needs and those of the team. Whilst this can entail consideration of further formal training, it should also be related to less formal activities such as 'time out' to read policies and procedures or being guided to other workers who have experience and understanding that could prove helpful for learning.

The *supportive and enabling* element is recognition of the inherently stressful nature of social work and the need to reduce any pressures that impair workers' ability to give effective help. It should entail the supervisor creating an enabling environment for the worker to let off steam and to explore their concerns, be it in relation to themselves, the service users or the agency. In effect, the supportive and enabling element should be about providing a forum for debriefing in which workers feel safe to express their thoughts and feelings. However, this is not only about talking and should involve supervisors also looking at ways of taking the stress out of a situation. Thompson (2002) describes this element as 'staff care' and reminds us of the pressure and stress that many workers face on a day-to-day basis. The supportive role should also include issues of personal safety and the need for self-protection, including the management of stress.

What these elements highlight is that effective supervision contains many of the elements of good practice with service users. It is also open to be influenced by the gender, personality and approaches of both parties, as well as the demands of the work setting. For supervision to be successful, it requires the commitment of all concerned, none more so than the worker. The worker's role in supervision is often viewed as passive, responding to the agenda of the supervisor. In our experience this is a recipe for disaster, leading to the disempowerment of the worker in relation to the agency and also has the potential to be both oppressive and discriminatory. It provides a poor role model for subsequent work with service users. Workers need to give consideration to their roles and responsibilities in the process and how they are able to create a positive and empowering relationship. At the very least this means that they have to be organised and give consideration to negotiating how the process is managed, including what they expect from supervisors (Thompson 2002).

The Role of the Tutor and Practice Teacher

Supervision is also a key aspect of the relationship between the student, practice teacher and tutor. One of the greatest challenges for social work educators is to enable students to develop a blueprint for future supervisory interactions that are positive and empowering (Watson and West 2003). There are two important areas within the supervisory process that students can begin to identify and respond to – how they learn to integrate theory and practice in a manner that informs their ongoing work and how they respond to the power dynamics within the supervisory relationship. Students frequently raise concerns about their ability to integrate theory and practice, fearing that they are being tokenistic, using theory for theory's sake. Many find themselves on practice placements where the use of theory tends to be implicit or there appears to be no clear consensus about what it constitutes. Consequently, they are often unclear about its place within their practice, leaving them with 'an ambivalent relationship with theory' (Preston-Shoot and Agass 1990, p. 5). This can lead to a situation where on the one hand they are searching for concrete knowledge to evidence competence and on the other struggling to use this formal learning in the complexity and uncertainty of practice. It is not helped by much of their academic learning being developed context-free and therefore distant from practice or the emphasis on 'doing ' rather than 'thinking' within the culture of many organisations.

The dynamics of the relationships between students, tutors and practice teachers tend to lend themselves to an uneven power dynamic which can make it more difficult for students to be active participants in their own learning (Hackett and Marsland 1997). This perceived power imbalance is reinforced by traditional approaches to learning and teaching which place the teacher as the 'expert' and the student in the role of passive learner. This, in our view, is an unhelpful and inappropriate model for social work education within both the academic context and the practice environment. By adopting an adult learning model, students are encouraged to be active participants in their own learning, questioning and challenging not only their own perceptions but also those of other workers. By adopting an essentially constructivist approach to learning, tutors can explore with students situations in which they can safely think and reflect on their practice in terms of what is happening and what has happened. Using the tutorial relationship and process in this way is not a simple and straight-forward activity. However, if we are able to create experiences where these dilemmas can be overcome, i.e. concrete and practical activities, reflection can facilitate 'inquiry, criticism, change and accountability' (Fook 1996, p. 5). In this context, tutorials can become what Ruch (2000, p. 107) describes as a 'sense-making forum, offering the opportunity to test out the congruence between theoretical understanding and lived realities'. This process, if replicated within the practice context, can enable students to take this participatory model with them into their future supervisory situations as new workers, thereby offering them an alternative to an organisational culture of 'theoryless practice'. It will also assist new workers in modelling a similar response to service users, ensuring that they are actively involved in the development of solutions to their difficulties. It would be our view that unless workers can to some extent 'manage their managers', they are unlikely to be able to create an empowering context for service users. This is particularly important within the increasingly integrated approach to service delivery, where service users are required to interact with an increasingly diverse range of professionals.

Working with Others: Skill for Professional Practice

Recent years have witnessed a growing collaboration between agencies in the health and social care field (Bradley and Manthorpe 2000). This has occurred because of the number of enquiries highlighting how service users have fallen between the gaps in service provision, often to disastrous effect. What this implies for workers is that they have to be aware of the potential and limitations this brings to practice. Different professional groups have different agendas and values bases that not only impact on their work with service users, but also reflect in the relationships they develop (Banks 2004). While many explanations have been offered for the difficulties in developing a seamless transition for service users between the many agencies they encounter, the fact that workers come from very different ethical and professional traditions is undoubtedly a factor. In terms of service provision for older people, for example, many of the workers providing direct services – district nurses, physiotherapists, community psychiatric nurses – do so based on a medical model of health and wellbeing. The assessments they make are likely to be restricted to aspects of functionality related to their own discipline: whether the service user can wash and dress unaided; whether there are ways in which the service user's mobility can be improved. The underlying assumption is that the 'expert' worker has the skills necessary to 'diagnose' the problem and effect a solution with minimal involvement of the service user. Social workers and perhaps occupational therapists are more likely to evaluate the situation using a social model of health that attempts to assess people within their social situation using a holistic approach to assessment. Within this perspective, service users are viewed as being the experts in their own lives and therefore more likely to be involved in the process of developing appropriate solutions. For service users, these differing emphases can be problematic and can lead to contradictory approaches and at times duplication of service provision. Acknowledgement of the difficulties has led in recent years to a growing integration of agencies to provide a more seamless service (Office of the Deputy Prime Minister 2004).

In the present social policy climate of interprofessional working, with single shared assessments, rationalisation of service provision, etc., it is becoming increasingly difficult for particular professional groups to demarcate their territory. Indeed, it is clear from the wider social policy context that greater integration of professional tasks is seen as the way forward. This is evidenced by guidance issued in relation to community care services in Scotland that explains the benefits of joint working:

> For professionals: the opportunity to break down cultural and other barriers, to develop a better understanding of others' skills, and to develop a wider range of personal skills to serve users, patients and carers.
>
> For front-line staff: the opportunity to develop a wider skill base, to meet more effectively needs of individual users, patients and carers, and support them to live the life they want. (Scottish Executive 2001)

Against this social policy context, it is important for social workers to be able to identify their role while working creatively with workers from different disciplines in order to ensure effective service delivery. Working in a collaborative manner requires an ability to appreciate the perspectives of others while not necessarily endorsing them. As indicated earlier, workers from different disciplines do not necessarily draw upon the same ideological framework and may not share a common understanding of terminology (Runciman 1989; Banks 2004). This can potentially lead to problematic relationships as workers strive to provide their interpretation of a quality service. Social workers do, however, have the skills to respond effectively to this situation, bringing to it a clear anti-oppressive perspective. This can be illustrated by looking again at Sandeep and his family. In order for Sandeep to be able to return home and lead as independent a life as possible, he would need to work with a number of different professionals, each likely to have his or her own perspective on his needs. As the coordinator of the situation, the social worker would have the opportunity to facilitate this process in a way that enabled Sandeep and his family to be active participants.

Partnership is a key element in the process for Sandeep, not just in terms of his own inclusion in the decision-making but also to facilitate effective partnerships between workers. This might involve the worker in discussions with others about how they could effectively coordinate their work to cause the least possible disruption to the life of the family. Such discussions could range from the simple process of ensuring that visits were not duplicated to the more complex task of ensuring that planning took account of Sandeep's views and reflected a social model of health care. The social worker should work towards building on the strengths of other workers while respecting their professional autonomy in order to achieve the best possible outcome for the family.

By *networking* across the agencies involved, the worker could begin to build effective working relationships and learn more about the organisational issues that might impose constraints on service delivery. The range of professional disciplines involved with Sandeep, at the point of discharge from hospital, would work within different organisational structures and have differing processes of accountability. This would be likely to impose particular constraints on their autonomy and their flexibility of response. Workers need to develop an understanding of these issues to be able to work effectively with other professionals. As with the more familiar process of mapping the social networks of service users, workers would need realistically to appraise the ability of particular individual service providers to contribute to Sandeep's care plan.

Flexibility of approach is therefore important if collaboration is to be effective. This does not, however, mean unnecessary compromise or capitulation. It is about responding realistically to what is being offered and being flexible enough to adjust plans where this becomes necessary. It might be, for example, that the worker would wish all the adaptations to Sandeep's home to be completed before his return. A judgement might, however, need to be made about the timing of this return home if a particular aspect of the work could not be completed within the agreed timescale. Sandeep might be prepared to return home before the new downstairs bedroom had been completed, feeling that he was willing to trade the inevitable chaos for the pleasure of being within his own family unit.

One of the dangers inherent in a multi-agency approach is that a degree of *collusion* begins to emerge between the workers to the detriment of the service user's perspective. This can emerge from an eagerness on the part of workers to be seen to be sharing a common set of objectives and for the relationships to be working well. Within this context, challenge is rare, as workers develop a common perception of the difficulties that they confront. This can lead to the externalising of difficulties into the service user. Sandeep could, for example, be seen as difficult to please within such a situation where the inability of workers appropriately to challenge each other was transferred to him. Instead of challenging the worker who had not fulfilled the agreed contract, it would be Sandeep who was viewed as 'too demanding'.

Monitoring and evaluation are vital elements of interdisciplinary work as it is important to monitor work undertaken against agreed targets. Again, the worker's anti-oppressive stance should ensure that any such evaluation takes full account of the service user's perspective and is not tokenistic in its approach. This would require the worker to incorporate an understanding of the cultural and social factors which impacted on Sandeep's rehabilitation, and service delivery should be monitored for signs of institutional racism or gender bias. Working within a multi-agency context poses particular challenges for workers but can be viewed as an extension of core social work skills. Perhaps the most crucial contribution by social work is the articulation of a person-centred, holistic approach to assessment of need, which can be a very effective counterbalance to the medicalisation of difficult situations.

Summary of Chapter

1. Reflective practice is a skilled activity that is dependent on a number of factors, including the ability of workers to develop their skills and knowledge within a supportive agency context.

2. It provides a means for workers to increase their understanding of both their own approach and the situation faced and experienced by service users. This implies reflecting *in* action and *on* action, activities that, whilst problematic, can influence and enhance both current and future practice. A number of practical tools can be used to facilitate this, including process recordings reflective diaries, critical incident analysis, and personal learning audits.

3. Good practice is a planned and purposeful activity that needs to be constantly evaluated and reflected upon by both the worker and the agency. The forum for this for most workers is supervision, which also should consider factors such as agency accountability and support.

Empowering and supportive supervision helps enable workers to develop good practice.

4. There is a range of skills involved in working with other professionals and agencies including partnership, networking, flexibility and monitoring and evaluation in a multidisciplinary agency where there are differing agendas and values influencing the aims of intervention.

9

Evaluation of Practice: Learning for the Future

Social work practice is increasingly rooted in the need to justify intervention in terms of effectiveness and efficiency and whether value for money has been achieved. For most workers this becomes enmeshed in audited systems of measuring the tangible outcomes of service delivery. It is about demonstrating the extent to which agency targets have been achieved – which may be very different from the service experienced by the user. However, whilst part of the managerial agenda, evaluation is also integral to good professional practice, enabling workers to learn from their experiences and to enhance the quality of service being delivered. Given the potential scope for discussion about the concept of evaluation, this chapter seeks to focus on the impact of evaluation on the work of individual practitioners as they interact with service users. It is not about research per se but rather is focused on the more reflective aspects of evaluation.

At a practice level, evaluation is a subjective activity informed, among other things, by the experience of workers, their understanding of the professional role, how they view the situation in question, their value stance and the requirements of the agency. As Everitt and Hardicker (1996, p. 25) state, evaluation 'involves making judgments about the "good". It is a value laden and political process and an important part of the repertoire of the professional practitioner.'

In this respect, it is unlikely that any two workers will evaluate a situation in exactly the same way, as can be seen in relation to John's situation described earlier. The workers who had seen him as part of the 'duty' system felt that they had successfully carried out the purpose of their intervention by dealing with John's presenting problems and ensuring that his immediate contact with the agency had been kept to a minimum. They were arguably adopting a procedural approach that focused primarily on the requirements of the agency. This was not the stance adopted by the worker who saw John on his sixteenth visit to the office and whose assessment of the situation was that it was more complex than just the presenting issues. 'Success' for this worker, from an individual pathology approach, was not about dealing with the immediate situation but was about enabling John to develop new ways of coping. This illustrates how it is possible to have the same situation but different assessments, actions and outcomes. There is unlikely, therefore, to be any consensus among workers about how 'success' should be evaluated.

Given the potential for different interpretations of the same events, it is important that workers have a clear sense of what they hope to achieve (outcome) and how this might happen (process). If evaluation is to occur in an empowering way, such events need to be interpreted in a manner that is inclusive of the service users' experiences (Dullea and Mullender 1999). Within a managerial culture, organisations are likely to interpret outcomes as the main measure of success through the use of mechanisms such as performance indicators, standards, etc. These are often imposed 'top-down' and therefore potentially disempowering (Watson 2002). Evaluation, in terms of outcome, is concerned more with quantifying the result of intervention. It answers the question of whether the agreed goals have been achieved and to what extent. In this context, there is an assumption that the current situation can be measured against what has gone before for the service user. Outcome evaluation would be more concerned, for example, about whether Tarjinder had ceased truanting and had returned to school than it would be with exploring the nature of the learning experience within the school for that young person. Where, for example, a behavioural method of intervention has been used, this presupposes the creation of targets as part of the methodology. Service users will be encouraged to identify concerns that require to be addressed, and the extent to which change is effected will determine the 'success' of the intervention. If goals were not achieved, why not? Were they set too high? Were they inappropriate? Were they properly negotiated? Evaluating outcome is by no means an easy task and raises all sorts of issues about who is the arbiter of 'success'. With the growth in interdisciplinary and agency work, the evaluative task becomes complicated by different attitudes, values and approaches to practice that may be difficult to reconcile.

The worker's evaluation of outcomes based on agreed goals is likely to be the starting point for any evaluative process. However, this can either be an ongoing part of the empowerment process with the service user or an activity undertaken by the worker to meet his or her own needs or those of the agency. Empowering practice from a democratic perspective requires the service user's opinions to be actively sought in relation to both process and outcome. This would include his or her experiences of the intervention, the part played by the worker and what they had learned and could use in the future, as well as whether their situation had improved in the way they thought it would. Empowering evaluation is about ensuring that this part of the process is undertaken, thereby enabling not just the worker but also the service user to learn for the future. Differences of opinion are as important as similarities, as they will compel us to rethink our assumptions about what happened and what was achieved. It is only by doing this in an open and positive manner that we will challenge and change our own practice.

Whilst outcome measurement is an important aspect of evaluation, it is equally valid to examine the means by which such outcomes have been achieved. In terms of process of the work being undertaken, evaluation can provide answers to the questions 'why' and 'how' and therefore links closely to reflection. In order to develop a clearer sense of the effectiveness of intervention, workers need to begin to dissect their involvement. As discussed in Chapters 5 and 6, evaluation happens in a different way depending upon the method of intervention. Within a task-centred method, for example, it might well have been agreed in the initial contract that particular aspects of the situation would be evaluated at the end of the process and that a set of criteria, against which the process of intervention could be measured, would be agreed with the service uses.

For example:

- Was the service user supported appropriately in the tasks that he or she had been identified to undertake?

- Did the agreed sessions take place on time?

- Was the written agreement effective in dealing with unforeseen circumstances?

Process evaluation relates to the methods, skills and strategies adopted to secure a particular set of objectives or outcomes. Evaluation, therefore, in terms of process is reflective and self-critical; formative evaluation provides important ongoing information about the nature of the relationship between service user and worker:

- What method of intervention did I choose?

- Why did this particular situation lend itself to this method?

- What was it about *this* method that made it easier to connect with *this* service user?

- What skills were employed and how were they selected?

- What strategies were utilised to secure the desired outcome?

Evaluation also provides information about the progress of the work being undertaken. As workers, therefore, we are asking questions such as:

- What did we agree as the purpose of intervention?
- Which aspects of this can be evaluated?
- How can they be evaluated?
- Why are they being evaluated?
- Who will evaluate them?
- Who will have primary responsibility for collating information?
- For what purpose will the information be used?

By working with the service user to develop evaluation criteria, we are indicating a willingness to be transparent about the purposes for which the outcome may be used. In situations where the reason for involvement arises out of some statutory responsibility, it is important that the end use of the evaluation be clear from the outset. Developing an inclusive approach to evaluation can help to consolidate empowering practice for both worker and service user. It is about growth and learning taking place within a context of openness and honesty as a model for future conduct by both parties. Brian's situation provides a useful example of this process.

The worker was asked to meet with Brian to review his situation after three months of his probation order had passed. Utilising a partnership approach meant that this process of formative evaluation needed to be clear from the outset and Brian needed to be fully involved.

By clarifying the *reasons for your involvement*, you would provide Brian with an opportunity to review his own contribution to the situation. If he were to begin to tackle the difficulties he faced, he might need to be reminded of the behaviour that caused him to be placed on probation. This is not always easy to achieve as service users may minimise the original reason for referral once they are at some distance from the event itself. Having established that your relationship arose out of Brian's court appearance, it would then become possible to work on the next stages of the process.

What could we agree to evaluate? It might be possible to agree to evaluate only some aspects of Brian's current situation. He might not, for example, have reached a point in his relationship with you where he was able to examine his use of alcohol but might be able to discuss his history of violence or his employment status. He might also wish to evaluate the extent to which he had found your intervention helpful.

How could these issues be evaluated? It might be that specific targets had been set. Brian's unemployment might be being tackled by another agency that had particular expectations of him. He might, for example, be expected to attend a job club on a set number of occasions per week. He might be attending an anger-management course. It would be possible, therefore, to agree on evaluative measures. Would you be agreeing to measure the raw data of attendance or would you be looking to evaluate the less tangible aspects such as participation, enthusiasm, etc.? Evaluating the usefulness of your intervention might take place at a fairly subjective level but it might be possible to tease out specific aspects which had been either helpful or not.

Why were these the issues to be evaluated? Brian might need to be reassured that the focus of the evaluation was to chart progress to date rather than to reach any final conclusions about the outcomes of intervention. It might be important, for example, to state clearly that, even in the event of a fairly negative evaluation, a breach of the probation order would not be sought at this stage. If his progress towards rebuilding his life were being hampered by the difficulties in your professional relationship, this would need to be examined.

Who would evaluate? If you were adopting a participative and inclusive approach, it would be vital for Brian to have an involvement in the process of evaluation. It would be likely to be helpful to his own skills if he were encouraged to help assess whether intervention in his life was proving to be beneficial. This would require him to be much more fully involved in the process of change that was taking place.

Who would be responsible for collating the information and how would it be used? Given that the nature of your involvement with Brian was as a result of a statutory responsibility, it would be necessary for you to retain records of any review of Brian's situation. This would need to be clearly explained and information would need to be provided about how such retained information might be utilised later. If, for example, Brian's progress were evaluated as being below expectations at this stage, then the formative evaluation might be used at a later date, alongside other similar evaluations, to form a recommendation in respect of the probation order.

By approaching evaluation in this way, information can be accumulated not just about the change process for the service user but also about the way in which the worker has impacted on his situation. This provides information that workers can utilise to develop their practice.

What is likely to sit alongside evaluation is a monitoring and review structure within the organisation that seeks to accumulate information about broader aspects of the work. Monitoring and review fulfils an important function in the development of social work services and it should be structured in a manner which facilitates change and, where necessary, improvement. With the increasing awareness of the importance of providing quality services at the lowest cost, social work services have been subjected to processes of auditing both internal and external (Adams 1998a). The monitoring of social work services tends to be focused on the tangible, quantifiable elements of provision rather than those that are more abstract. Most organisations now operate some form of computerised data-collection system into which details about individual pieces of work are entered in a codified manner. This allows for the analysis of the trends, the collation of statistics and other forms of raw data collection. While appreciating the value of such systems, they are often experienced by workers as unconnected to the professional task and therefore of less importance. They can, however, provide a rich source of data that may help workers understand more clearly the broader context of their work (Sermeus 2003). Having an awareness, for example, that schools within an area have high levels of absenteeism among pupils may help explain the response of an individual head teacher to a request to take a young person like Tarjinder with a history of truancy into the school. As has been discussed elsewhere, monitoring of services is required in order to generate evidence of performance relating to agreed National Standards frameworks. These processes are far from straightforward in their structures or delivery, as Adams et al. (2002, p. 287) suggest, 'Quality and quality assurance are contested concepts whose application is as deeply enmeshed as any aspect of social work in the politics of its management.' There are, however, monitoring processes which have a much more direct link to individual practice, e.g. case reviews. Here workers are frequently working within parameters set by legislative requirements. Reviews of children 'looked after' by the local authority need to take place within specified time frames and have fixed elements within their terms of reference. These requirements exist in response to concerns about 'drift' in the planning process for children (Rowe and Lambert 1973; DHSS 1985) and it is important to engage with them as evaluative opportunities rather than as a managerial imperative.

Whilst acknowledging the possibilities that exist in formal frameworks of evaluation, their propensity to set the parameters for what is considered important emphasises what is effective rather than what is ethical (Shaw and Lishman 1999). They are also based on the assumption that one set of criteria can fit all situations and that this then needs to be applied by workers to create evidence of 'what works'. This can be a narrow perspective that may be disempowering for the worker, denying consideration of their lived experience of the process, and it underplays activities that are crucial to reflection. An important part of professional practice is that workers also take responsibility for evaluation, shaping it in a way that reflects practice not just agency needs to justify measurable outcomes. As Cheetham and Kazi (1998, p.23) state, 'testing of hypotheses and critical scrutiny of theory and "practice wisdom", pursued energetically and with discipline, are as much part of evidence-based practice as "empirical practice" which seeks to capture particular outcomes, often using some standardized measurement tools'. Although single case evaluation is at an early stage of development, our assessment is that it is increasingly proving a useful tool for workers in enabling them to develop frameworks for evaluation that reflect professional concerns about process as well as effectiveness.

Single Case Evaluation

Single case evaluation refers to 'the use of single case designs by practitioners to evaluate client progress or the effectiveness of a system' (Kazi 1998, p.1). When first explored by Bloom and Fischer (1982) in the USA, this methodology was seen as offering practitioners the ability to evaluate the progress of intervention with service users. It was viewed as a means of systematically identifying what was successful in terms of intervention in order that this could be replicated elsewhere. Viewed as a method of incorporating research into direct practice, Fischer's initial response was one of considerable optimism for the potential impact on practice outcomes. He saw it as an accessible research tool that would greatly enhance the ability of individual workers to engage in research with service users. This has not been borne out in practice, however, as relatively few practitioners regularly evaluate their interventions in this way. Part of the reason for this, as Kazi (1998) points out, is that the model was overly concerned in its initial phase with looking for empirical evidence and consequently became reductionist rather than reflecting the complexity of social work relationships and practice. In this respect the model does have the potential to impose structure rather than reflect the uncertainty that workers face in reality. However, recent adaptations of single case evaluation have moved beyond this narrow approach to look at lived experiences and build in the need for reflection and process as well as outcome. In addition, the model has moved on from being worker/'expert'-driven to include partnership between workers and service users, thereby developing it as a potentially empowering way of evaluating practice. It is for these reasons that we feel that it can prove a useful tool, although we would add a cautionary note: it is not a 'one size fits all' framework but needs to be developed and used imaginatively by workers to fit the practice realities of the work as well as the service user's situation.

The basic framework for single case evaluation is a relatively simple and straightforward process to understand. The difficulty is applying it in an empowering way that reflects the uniqueness of each new situation. The first stage is to establish a baseline for intervention against which future work can be compared and measured. This comparison will be made both with the workers' own experiences of practice employed in similar situations and wider research in the field. Kazi (1998, p. 20) states: 'Baselining consists of collecting information about the magnitude or severity of the client's problem during a period prior to the onset of treatment [sic].' From this it is assumed that some prediction can be made about the likely level of progress to provide an indicator of potential change. Having established the baseline, it is then possible to decide how many stages are likely to be required within the overall design to secure the necessary outcomes. The most basic form of single case design is AB where A is the baseline and B is the point at which outcomes are evaluated. However, it is possible within the framework to have interim stages that are assessed and lead towards the completed goal. Clearly such a design cannot be analysed using complex variables and therefore provides fairly straightforward 'chicken and egg' analyses. This, however, does not necessarily negate its usefulness as an evaluative tool. It can be used to enable service users to take more control over their lives by providing a joint forum for discussion about what is to be achieved, how this will be done and what would be considered appropriate goals. If this is done alongside the service users it provides a framework for partnership working that enables those receiving the service to be part of the evaluative process.

If we look back at Susan, who was first encountered in Chapter 1, we can begin to identify how this evaluative process could be used. Susan, in this process, would be encouraged to discuss the issues in her life that prevented her from effectively parenting her children. She would be likely to identify as contributory factors:

● poor housing

● inadequate financial resources

● poor physical health.

From this information, it would be possible to predict and agree with Susan some likely outcomes based on intervention:

● Accessing more suitable accommodation would allow the family more physical space in which to live with each other.

● Assisting her to negotiate with relevant agencies might increase her income, thereby allowing some of the pressure of debt to be lifted.

● Supporting Susan to seek appropriate medical support for her depression might provide her with greater energy with which to respond to her children.

Each of these elements of Susan's situation could be examined to establish a baseline (A) from which progress could be measured. In terms of the issue of poor housing the likely baseline would be that Susan had been advised that she could not be rehoused because she was in arrears with her rent. The exact financial amounts could be recorded as part of the baseline documentation, together with details of current housing agency responses to her situation. The baseline of the evaluation (A) might therefore be: 'Rent arrears £200, housing agency unwilling to agree to anything other than full payment.' The purpose of recording this information would be to enable both Susan and the worker to retain an accurate account of the situation prior to intervention.

This would enable the process of evaluation to be more accurately undertaken. This could be charted as follows and a copy retained for reference by both Susan and the worker.

Did Susan secure more suitable accommodation? A record of process

Date	Nature of Intervention	Result
2 February	Susan completed application form for change of tenancy	Advised that rent arrears would be need to be cleared
11 February	Susan contacted benefits agency to request a loan	Awaited
23 February	Letter from benefits agency	Request declined
1 March	Advocacy by social worker with benefits agency	Agreement reached for weekly deduction of rent plus small payment towards arrears in principle
11 March	Housing authority agreed to process transfer request	

Having reached a point where the application was to be pursued by the housing agency, the worker would be able to explore with Susan how her situation had changed (the evaluation stage B). Both would be able to examine the process of change and to make an assessment of the relative importance of the contribution of both the worker and Susan. It would become a fairly straightforward process of evaluation to calculate by how much the arrears had been reduced and also the extent of personal advocacy and contacting of external agencies that Susan had been able to undertake. This would also allow for judgements to be made about the relative importance of both Susan and the worker to the process of change. This secondary evaluation would be likely to provide valuable insights into Susan's wider coping strategies. A similar pattern could be utilised to work on the issues raised by other elements of the initial assessment. For example:

● *Were her financial problems addressed?* – Log kept of income increases received and bills paid.

● *Was she feeling better?* – Diary kept by Susan to record her ability to motivate herself on a daily basis.

In this way it is possible to build up a systematic picture of how Susan's situation had changed over time and to explore the extent to which particular aspects of intervention had improved the situation overall. What it does not seek to do is to provide evidence as to the causality of the changes. It might well be that the changes in Susan's health status, for example, occurred as a consequence of a 'natural' improvement in her condition rather than any direct intervention. The measurable outcome for this purpose was, however, that over time her ability to motivate herself improved, and this can be evidenced from her diary.

Single case evaluation is not necessarily suitable for every worker in every situation. It does, however, have some advantages:

● It encourages a systematic exploration of the aims of intervention.

● It can enable service users to evaluate their own situation.

● It is a fairly simple methodology which can be used within practice.

● It potentially offers a mechanism whereby practitioners can be accountable to service users.

● It can assist the selection of an appropriate method of future intervention (Kazi 1998).

Single case designs allow the issues of concern to be broken down into agreed manageable tasks that can then be systematically evaluated. For some service users, this provides a much clearer understanding of the nature of their role within the change process and tends to prevent the creation of 'hidden agendas'. Utilising this method of intervention enables service users to have a clear understanding of the specific aspects of their situation that are being evaluated and also is transparent about the baseline from which 'success' will be measured. In terms of workers, it enables them to consider what situations have been changed and provides a starting point for reflecting upon their practice in terms of what lessons can be learned to develop good practice, identifying the commonalties in their 'successful ' practice or alternatively those in which they feel their impact has been limited.

Termination: A Partnership Approach

The final stage of the social work process is termination, an area of practice that has received relatively little attention in the literature (Coulshed and Orme 1998). Arguably this reflects the difficulties in determining the achievement of goals with many service users, as the complexity and change characteristic of their situation may mean that success is problematic to assess and therefore is at best partial. This often leaves the worker to make decisions about closing cases whilst a level of risk and uncertainty about future coping skills remain. However, in these days of heavy workloads and constant demand for the service, appropriate termination has become a key task, ensuring that those most in need or at risk are given an appropriate service. As Thompson (2002, p. 224) rightly points out, termination 'is more than a simple matter of tying up loose ends'. How we end our interventions can be as crucial as how we entered them and therefore need to be systematically considered in relation to the overall process of our work. Termination should be a planned part of the social work process, and should therefore provide all parties the opportunity and time to prepare for the future. Evaluation is a useful tool in the termination stage, enabling the service user and the worker to be reminded of timescales and deadlines and to reiterate what has been achieved and learned for future use. It can be a positive experience, acknowledging increasing skills and self-esteem that can be used after social work intervention has ended.

Some methods, like the task-centred approach, make clear statements about the time-limited nature of social work intervention and create a focus for endings right from the start. However, as we have seen in Chapter 6, this does not mean that longer-term intervention cannot be used in a way that has clear and delineated endings, although the emphasis may be different, particularly in the earlier stages of the work. Therefore, regardless of the particular method of intervention being used, it is important that the preparation for termination of the worker's involvement be carefully and sensitively constructed. This is an activity that is much easier to achieve if the work has been systematic and has had clear goals, as this will lend itself to clarity about what has been achieved and the subsequent endings of intervention. However, despite the best of intentions, ending intervention can be difficult to achieve for both the worker and the service user (Coulshed and Orme 1998).

Endings are not always possible to plan in advance: workers may have to transfer service users before the completion of the agreed work for a variety of reasons such as obtaining a new job, altered caseload-management priorities or the end of statutory involvement; service users may no longer have a statutory obligation to see the worker, they may feel that they have done enough to move on or they may have physically relocated to another area (Thompson 2002). This does not mean that the termination phase can be ignored, but it needs to be structured to reflect these realities. Transfer of work provides a useful example. Service users often need to be reassured about the implications for them of the introduction of a new worker. They may need to be reminded of the effectiveness of the work already undertaken and to be clear that they do not need to start again with the new worker. This can engender strong feelings in both the service user and the worker, who may both be reluctant to engage in a process of change. It is important to undertake an evaluation of the work already completed in order that service users can appreciate their own strengths and can begin to consider how these can be transferred into a new working relationship. It can be a useful boost to the self-esteem of workers to have service users imply that they will not be able to work with someone else, that they will not be able to re-create the rapport. If, however, workers are committed to an empowering approach, they should enable service users to transfer into a new working relationship. This process can be assisted by an exploration of the new skills that have been developed and perhaps by the worker and the service user sitting down together to write a transfer summary for the agency's records. It may also be appropriate to arrange for the new worker to be apprised of the situation in the service user's presence, thereby avoiding the need to cover old or possibly painful ground when they take up responsibility for the case (Coulshed and Orme 1998). It is not an activity that should be entered into lightly, therefore, but should be systematically and sensitively considered with the service user.

Endings are also difficult because intervention is not always as linear and logical a process as we might imagine. This can be affected by a number of factors including the complexity of the service user's situation, and issues of disorganisation and dependency. Lack of clarity about the purpose of intervention means that endings can become difficult to identify. Unless workers and service users are clear about what they have set out to achieve, it becomes more difficult to be clear about when the objectives have been reached. Potentially, this can lead to 'drift' that makes it increasingly difficult to agree when the work to be undertaken has ended. If, for example, the worker had not negotiated clear aims and objectives with Brian in relation to his probation order, it would be very easy to respond to every new issue that arose and make it difficult to decide when the work had ended. This lack of clarity can leave the worker at the mercy of future events which may be of concern, creating a situation of uncertainty for both worker and service user. Dependency, on the other hand, means that both workers and service users feel unable to move on, as they have become reliant on the support provided. Termination in this situation becomes particularly problematic, as the worker will be faced with either leaving the service user unprepared for the future or continuing work that is no longer seen as crucial (Thompson 2002). Dependency is as likely to be problematic for workers as it is for service users. Having built up a relationship over time with service users, workers may find it difficult to terminate involvement because of the degree of personal commitment they have developed. John, for example, being an affable and engaging man was able to form good relationships with the workers involved with him and they soon began to provide him with emotional as well as practical support. Given his situation as an older male, living alone with few personal supports, workers became drawn into a process of nurturing and supporting him. It is often difficult for workers in this situation to appreciate the extent to which they are meeting their own needs within this relationship as well as those of the service user. The service user's situation may, to some extent, mirror the worker's own life experiences and thereby trigger a series of responses. Reflecting upon one's practice and making appropriate use of supervision to evaluate one's intervention can be valuable means of evaluating any dependency that has developed and formulating a planned and structured process of disengagement (Ruch 2000). Undertaking such work with John might include some discussion with him about the skills he possessed in terms of relationship-building. By exploring with him the way in which he had been able to impact upon the professionals who had met him the worker can help to build John's belief in himself as a skilled communicator who found it fairly easy to engage with others. When discussing the termination of social work intervention, it would therefore be important to enable John to examine how these skills could be transferred into other contexts.

Finally, termination cannot be excluded from the change process, as while endings may create opportunities they can also lead to fear, anxiety and loss (Coulshed and Orme 1998). This is true for both workers and service users who can be equally resistant to change, sticking to the familiar even when it has lost its purpose. It is for this reason that people need to know where they stand and can negotiate what is expected, enabling them to take control over the change process (Handy 1993). Endings for Susan, for example, had often been traumatic and unsatisfactory. She had experienced the sudden departure of significant people throughout her life. Terminating a working relationship with Susan would therefore require taking account of this prior experience and enabling her to control the pace of the ending as far as possible.

The Worker: Knowledge and Skills for Good Practice

Throughout this text we have emphasised that the knowledge and skills required for practice will be influenced by the service user's situation, the worker's approach and agency and statutory requirements. Arguably, there is no definitive knowledge or skills for good practice that can be utilised on all occasions, as each situation is unique. This is not to suggest that social work is an activity devoid of knowledge and skills, rather that the complexity and uncertainty of the task means that there are no definitive statements that can be made. These difficulties are compounded by the contested nature of what social work should be aiming to achieve, as this will clearly impact on the knowledge and skill required. This debate has generated heated discussion in social work education about what aspiring practitioners need to learn and what should be the balance between the competing demands in this context. Arguably, educators have tried to put the quart into the pint pot with the consequent outcome that workers have breadth but not depth in relation to what is required to practise. In particular this would appear to leave new workers feeling that there is a skills gap that they have to bridge on qualification that was not met during their education (Marsh and Triseliotis 1996). What has become increasingly clear in recent years, partially as a result of this debate, is that good practice is both a 'thinking' and a 'doing' activity that has purpose and needs to be planned and organised. In addition, 'thinking' and 'doing' are not separate but interrelated activities that draw on skills influenced by both formal and experiential knowledge.

Whilst we considered practice knowledge and theories for practice in Chapter 2 and how these were influenced by the worker's approach, we feel it is important to develop some key points made throughout the text. In this respect we are not trying to produce the definitive audit of what workers need to know but provide a starting point from which to build practice. Good practice requires workers to have knowledge to enable them to understand the 'person in situation' (Hollis 1972). In effect it is about understanding both the sociological (society and community) and psychological (personality and life span) and how these interrelate and impact on the service user (Howe 1987). The former is important as it is about locating the individual in the opportunities that exist and the oppressions that have impacted on their lives. The latter is important because it helps workers understand how individuals have responded to their experiences and how they will be able to face the challenges and concerns of their situation. This will also be dependent on obtaining knowledge about the cultural aspects of the situation and what this means in terms of the support networks that can be utilised, including families and friends. However, as we have already stated, the service user also needs to be located in the agency and statutory context of the service that is to be delivered. They need to have an understanding of the organisation and its legal responsibilities and how these are delivered and can be adapted to meet the service user's needs. Workers also require an understanding of the limits to their professional discretion, and what supports they can personally expect in their work (Braye and Preston-Shoot 1995). What should be apparent, even at the most cursory glance, is that this formal knowledge is constantly changing, which means that workers need to update themselves regularly in these areas.

One of our concerns about present practice is that it is often reduced to an event or a series of events determined and shaped by procedures which are allegedly applied in a 'technical' manner. The danger with this stance is that it can reinforce oppression by failing to recognise the structural nature of concerns and exclude service users from their own lives. Social work is rarely straightforward; it is a value-laden activity that is based on a process, a way of structuring our intervention, be it short- or long-term. Workers in this context need to have knowledge of both themselves and the range and type of interventions that are possibly applicable to their work. They require personal knowledge, particularly self-awareness, in order to understand how they and their approach are impacting on the service users' concerns and possible ways forward. They also require knowledge of the social work process so that services can be designed to fit the uniqueness of the service user and their situation, not just their own or agencies' needs. Finally, workers need to be able to develop their formal knowledge within the practice setting, learning from experience what works and what does not work. Whilst this will also involve learning from research and others' experience, it should include the workers' own practice, using reflection to build a range of knowledge, including the relevance of formal and practice knowledge that is applicable to their approach and skills (Fook 2002).

Good practice requires skills if it is to be effective. Once again there is no definitive list. However, Trevithick (2000) and Thompson (2002) provide a good starting point for understanding the main skills and how these can be applied in practice. In considering the following skills, we have tried to build upon those already considered in this text but often given little attention by workers. However, there are many that we could have highlighted which workers do use daily in a positive and empowering manner.

These would include skills such as interviewing, support, enabling and communication to name but a few. Given the range of possible skills required for practice – for example, Trevithick (2000) identifies fifty, and Thompson (2002) twenty – we have tried to emphasise those that we feel are important to both practice and process. Underpinning this text and a central skill for both effective and ethical practice is empowerment. Whilst we are aware that this is based on knowledge and values, it is also a skill that needs to be utilised in every aspect of our intervention across the social work process. How skilled we are will be crucial in terms of service users' investment in the work and will often mean the difference between informing and genuine partnership in practice. It is a skill that incorporates many of the others we have considered in this text, such as communication, listening, understanding and enabling.

If good practice is about being open and honest about what we can do, we need to examine the skill of negotiation. This is about finding ways of exploring what action is possible, given the realities of both the service user's and the worker's situation. Whilst underpinned by assessment and the skills which that involves, negotiation implies that good practice will not always be about achieving the ideal, but about finding the best possible way forward in any given situation. It requires that we acknowledge others' contributions and limitations as well as our own in the social work process (Coulshed and Orme 1998). Failure to use and develop negotiating skills invariably means someone has imposed his or her preferred solution on the situation and disempowered or oppressed others, often the service user, as a result.

Decision-making is another skill that is frequently undervalued. If not used appropriately, this can lead to the service user being disadvantaged or excluded. Making decisions is integral to determining what action to take, in what way and why. In effect, decision-making is part of the social work process, starting from the first contact with the service user to the last. Workers constantly make decisions which impact on their own work setting and direct practice. Often these are made with limited information, with lack of certainty and with time and resource constraints. These are all factors which mean that decision-making has the potential to reflect the immediate needs of the worker or agency. Whilst workers will always be under pressure to make decisions, good practice means that this is, as O'Sullivan (1999) highlights, a systematic process based on all the available information, including the context of the situation and acknowledged feelings and facts, and involves the service user as far as possible. Our concern is that unless this is a conscious and deliberate activity for the worker, what will influence decision-making is our own bias and concerns, factors that can be detrimental to good practice.

If effective and ethical practice is an organised and purposeful activity then this is crucial in terms of how the worker conducts himself or herself.

Good practice is almost impossible to deliver in chaotic situations where workers have no control over the pressures of work (Thompson 2000). It was for this reason that we felt it was important to consider the use of time, personal organisation and workload management. These are all skills that can be enhanced by the worker. However, they often run against the reactive ethos of many organisations and workplace cultures (Jones 2001). Failure to use these skills often means that we imply to service users that they are not important or do not count. Failure to keep appointments or turning up late without any prior notice are illustrations of the prioritising of agency/personal needs. For service users, this can reinforce many of their previous life experiences of powerlessness and lead to them disengaging from the social work process. It may also mean that workers are unlikely to be able to practise in any planned or consistent manner as they are blown from one reactive situation to another. It is our contention that workers must accept responsibility for their professional practice but also need to attempt to ensure that this becomes part of the organisational culture. Managers, equally, need to accept responsibility for shaping the professional ethos of their services by promoting a 'learning culture' that is not about the attribution of blame. Unless such changes occur, there is little possibility of moving the professional agenda forward, as empowering effective practice will not happen and therefore will not be evidenced.

The last area we want to consider is reflection. As we have seen above, many of the skills needed for practice are often underutilised to the detriment and disempowerment of the service users. The skill of reflection should not just be related to our direct practice but to how we approach the task and also utilise our skills repertoire in that context. We can learn from all aspects of our experiences as workers and adapt and enhance these to develop practice, including negotiation and decision-making. However, this is dependent on us being able to reflect in an open and honest manner and challenge current practice. Reflection is the key to ensuring that our practice is based on empowerment for service users, not solely getting caught up in approaches that give greater emphasis to the worker or agency. This is likely to provide a more useful and accurate means of evaluating the worker's skill and the outcome of intervention.

Summary of Chapter

1. Evaluation is an integral part of the modern social work agenda, in terms of both effective and ethical practice. It relates to both process and outcome and to be empowering requires the active participation of service users throughout the process.

2. Recent years have seen the spread of formal organisational frameworks for the evaluation and monitoring of workloads. Whilst these agency frameworks are important and can be helpful, the professional agenda would suggest workers should also develop their own models of evaluation, particularly around practice. In this respect, Single Case evaluation is considered as a starting point to develop a 'simple' framework that can be applied to practice.

3. The last stage of the social work process is termination, an activity that is often understated in both the literature and reality of practice. Effective endings are important to ensure that the gains of intervention are not lost and that service users are able to maintain their more empowered and confident status. Termination, as with all stages, needs to be open, planned and shared with the service users if it is to see the empowerment and partnership stance of the worker carried to its logical conclusion.

4. Good practice is both a 'thinking' and a 'doing' activity which requires the worker to have appropriate knowledge and skills to put into practice. Whilst some knowledge and skills have obtained considerable attention, others, such as experiential knowledge and decision-making, have been underplayed. What is important is that the workers should be self-aware and able to build on their strengths in order to become more effective.

10

Conclusion: Approaches to Practice and Modern Social Work

As a socially constructed and contested occupation, social work is influenced by a myriad of factors that need to take account of the perspectives of the service user, worker, agency and society (Payne 1997). What this means for individual workers is that the backdrop to their practice will be influenced and constrained by the prevailing discourses about how social work should be organised and what it aims to achieve. The dominant discourse within the public and social services is that of managerialism related to the so-called 'modernisation agenda', with its claim to make services more competitive, efficient and customer-focused (Clarke and Newman 1997). Key to these developments is an 'agenda for action' which requires the development of plans and targets with specific dates for completion (Mitchell 2000). In the context of this narrative, two key concepts have been central to the debate about change: managers and markets. According to James (1994, p. 56), in this managerial discourse public organisations, including social services, 'are or should be, orderly set-ups where the best people are at the top and where everybody knows their place. Managing is primarily about achieving task, and the good manager is the one who directs people clearly and objectively to achieve that task.'

Implicit in this managerial discourse is the assumption that service delivery can be defined in a tangible manner (outcomes) that has meaning to workers in terms of their everyday practice. This is part of the reason why, over the last decade, there has been a growth in procedures, performance measures and standards. Procedures provide guidance as to how the task should be undertaken; performance measures and standards seek to ensure that it has been achieved to a satisfactory level. What has also run with this managerial discourse has been a push to break the monopoly of public services by the creation of markets for welfare. The argument in

165

favour of markets is a simple one; it is based on the competitive market where the free interplay of supply and demand will determine the price of goods or services (Bartlett and Le Grand 1993). Whilst there has been debate about the relevance of markets in relation to social work (Adams 1996), many services which were once the preserve of the local state are now provided by voluntary or private sectors. However, it is not the notion of markets that concerns us at this point in time but that of the service user's position in this analysis – the customer. Whilst there has been much debate about whether service users are customers in the traditional sense (Clarke and Newman 1997; Parrott 1999), it is what this concept means for the empowerment debate that is our main concern. Customers are afforded limited say in relation to how the service is provided and at best are able to walk away if it is not suitable. Whilst the latter is highly unlikely for many social work service users, what the managerial discourse promotes is a limited empowerment agenda, based less on the process of intervention (ethical) and more on what has been achieved (efficiency). In terms of good practice, empowerment in this discourse fits a limited individual agenda, that of informing rather than a more democratic perspective of working together in partnership.

The above changes have created an organisational environment conducive to the procedural approach and one that is relatively hostile to that of individual pathology. The congruence with the procedural approach is related to its claimed ability to meet achievable outcomes, usually around presenting problems. It is also heralded as an approach that provides clarity to workers who have had to make sense of the growing demands on an already-stretched service whose resources are limited. This fits with the practice wisdom in many work settings of keeping the show on the road by getting the job done. Work is said to be organised in a systematic manner designed by the worker who will keep the service user informed, though not necessarily involved in decision-making. Alternatively, the individual pathology approach, with its emphasis on more open-ended work, designed by the expert worker, now has limited meaning. Many social work organisations (particularly in the public sector) and some larger voluntary organisations have therefore adopted a procedural approach to practice, with workers providing pre-defined short-term responses, often using case management, task-centred or behavioural methods. The individual pathology approach, on the other hand, has increasingly been marginalised from mainstream provision; it now tends, in our experience, to be adopted within specialist projects in the public sector or is the preserve of smaller voluntary sector organisations. This is not to argue that some techniques within the individual pathology approach cannot fit the managerial agenda; clearly some forms of counselling can. However, the wider approach undoubtedly had difficulties meeting many of the demands made in relation to procedures, standards and the limited empowerment agenda.

Whilst the procedural approach has gained ascendancy in many social work organisations, this still leaves the question of its relevance to service users or the professional social work agenda. Our concern in relation to service users is that the quantitative stance taken in performance measurement can become particularly problematic in the personal social services (Drummond 1993; Adams 1996). The effectiveness of social work is based on more than the technical implementation of procedures with observable outcomes. The ethical component means that we also need to consider issues such as feelings, opinions and relationships. Effectiveness for many service users is often dependent upon the development or impact of relationships, which are subjective (Drummond 1993; Dickens 1995). Service users' past experiences can also impact on present circumstances and any approach that does not appropriately acknowledge this will be limited in its relevance. It is for this reason that we consider that elements of the individual pathology approach still have currency in the mainstream of provision, as long as they are underpinned with an empowering perspective. What this highlights is the difficulty of identifying quantifiable causes or predetermining outcomes from the complexity and uncertainty of many service users' situations.

The complexity of measuring and determining performance can be seen from the following simple scenario in relation to Tarjinder's school truancy. The work as we have seen, including causes and solutions, was not only about Tarjinder but also about his mother, Ravinder, and his father, Sandeep. Its success was dependent on the whole family's motivation, insight and desire to change. The worker's knowledge, skills and abilities also impacted on the situation, both positively and negatively. In addition, the school's approach and commitment to dealing with truancy were of importance. These are factors that are often outwith the worker's ability to influence directly or even indirectly. On the assumption that all these factors could be put in place, we are still left with the issue of how success would be determined in Tarjinder's situation. Success might involve:

● return to school

● partial return

● changing school

● attendance at an alternative social work provision.

These are issues and dilemmas that do not even consider the history of the situation or the more pervasive factors faced by Tarjinder and his family, such as poor health and discrimination. That apart, even at the oversimplified level of this scenario, it does highlight how difficult it is to measure and assess the success or otherwise of the service provided.

This complexity does not mean that performance measurement is an activity that should not be undertaken. What needs to be acknowledged is that it is more than looking at objective factors, as many services are also subjective in terms of their consequent outcomes (Munro 2001). These are factors which imply that performance measurement should be treated with caution rather than certainty. To fail to adopt a wider perspective, as is implicit in the procedural approach with its emphasis on surface issues, will miss many of the important aspects of the service, particularly around the service user/worker interface and what this means for good practice.

In terms of the professional agenda, arguably the procedural approach does not develop the concept of empowerment far enough to challenge the oppression and discrimination faced by many service users. Empowerment in this approach, as we have already argued, is often around enabling individuals to change their behaviour, either for their own or for society's benefit. If this is what service users desire, then it is hard to argue against this stance. However, within the procedural approach, empowerment is less inclined to acknowledge or challenge the power relationships reflected in the structure of service provision or society (Dalrymple and Burke 1995; Pugh and Thompson 1999). Empowerment is about locating service users within their social and historical context, and the oppression and inequality which can ensue from that situation (Braye and Preston-Shoot 1995). Achieving this form of empowerment is not something that occurs magically; it has to be worked upon to enable those being empowered to challenge the sources of their oppression. Dalrymple and Burke (1995) identify a four-stage model of the process towards empowerment, moving from the individual developing an awareness of the source of their disempowerment through to the development of political action and change. In this context, empowerment is about change with regard to the service user and change to the system and its present power relationships, rather than trying to make the system and its present culture and ethos more effective. Democratic empowerment, therefore, does not sit comfortably with an approach such as the procedural one that restricts service users to the role of customers and prescribes responses that are tightly defined around predetermined procedures with specified outcomes.

Whilst any approach will struggle to fit the competing discourses of the organisation, service user and professional, it is our view that workers have a responsibility to try to influence that debate by bridging the gap to good practice. What is important is not just seeking a compromise between the discourses and then determining what can be achieved, it needs workers to influence and challenge the context of their practice. In our view, the progressive approach has the most potential to provide effective and ethical practice. In terms of effectiveness, it acknowledges the need for practice that can be evidenced, although widens this out to include more subjective factors. Therefore, at the heart of the progressive approach is a political analysis centred on oppression and social justice, which seeks to empower service users to take control over their lives. It is based on a democratic empowerment agenda where service users are citizens rather than customers. The implication of this is that citizens should have a say in all aspects of the service, including how it is delivered, and not just the end product. The progressive approach and democratic empowerment agenda is increasingly obtaining a foothold in social work education, practice and service delivery as workers and some organisations struggle to move beyond the more defensive position of managerialism. However, this is a practice that is predicated on proving itself not just more empowering but more effective. A core theme throughout this text is that good practice needs to be evidenced and evaluated, rebutting the often-stated 'commonsense' claims of the progressive approach being more time-consuming or less effective than other approaches. Good practice is more organised, thorough, and dependent on a range of knowledge and skills to put into practice. It is also one that is based on continually learning, both formally and experientially, about our approach in order that we can ensure that the service user's situation is at the heart of practice.

Continuing Professional Development: The Key to Good Practice and Survival

Continuing professional development requires workers to maintain a level of involvement in current research and practice development, particularly within their area of expertise. This is not something that has a strong tradition in social work practice, where workers have at times made a virtue of 'theoryless' practice (Howe 1987). As noted earlier, some of the processes that aid reflection – learning logs, process recording, reflective diaries – are seen as being the primary preserve of the student rather than the qualified worker. The danger of this stance is that workers can become enmeshed in a reactive practice that responds mainly to outside pressures, such as the demands of the agency or service users. Good practice implies that workers are able to take control of their own situations, shaping and responding to service users' demands in an empowering manner. To work in a more proactive way is an intellectual activity that needs to be constantly honed and refined to meet the ever-changing and complex challenges of service delivery. It is our view that we short-change service users if we do not offer them a service based on the highest possible level of knowledge and skill. Providing this within the current culture of anti-intellectualism within social work organisations is not easy, although this is slowly changing. There are now increasing expectations of continuing professional development linked to worker' registration with relevant professional bodies charged with the responsibility for the maintenance of practice standards. This will require workers to demonstrate the specific means by which they have developed their knowledge and skills since the previous point of audit. This activity should be interpreted as an opportunity for workers to be supported in their learning within the workplace rather than as a set of administrative hoops to be jumped through. It also provides an opportunity to reaffirm the professional role and task of social work practice within an increasingly complex interdisciplinary environment where boundaries become blurred and workers can begin to feel deskilled (Bradley and Manthorpe 2000). If we are committed to working in an empowering way with service users, then this requires us also to empower ourselves by being as well-equipped as possible for the challenges of the practice environment.

Post–qualifying education takes many forms, some more formal than others. It can range from brief in-house sessions on specific issues to full courses with academic and professional accreditation. This can be achieved through critical reflection on practice or formal 'taught' knowledge within the academic environment. What is important for workers is that this should form part of a consistent approach to the professional task that places value on the intellectual skills they possess rather than implying that the 'doing' is more important. There are a number of ways in which workers can maintain the discipline of reflective practice within the context of busy social work agencies.

Maintaining some form of reflective journal. As indicated earlier, learning skills developed during training can be effectively utilised within the practice context. Having developed the ability to keep a reflective account of one's practice as a student, this can continue to be useful as a worker. By noting briefly any value dilemmas or conflicts that arise, concerns about agency demands, evidence of good practice, etc., workers can build up a valuable resource. This can be used as an aide-mémoire for supervision purposes or as a means of keeping track of personal development. It also helps to keep alive the skills of reflection and critical analysis.

Developing a supportive network within the workplace. This can help to create a structure to enhance practice skills. By sharing with colleagues, on a fairly informal basis, any concerns, triumphs or points of information, the overall skills and knowledge of the group can be developed. With the ever-increasing pace of change within the social work environment, it is not possible for every practitioner to be fully conversant with every development. It also provides opportunities for workers to explore values issues and to collectively challenge oppression within the workplace.

Action Learning Sets. These provide opportunities for colleagues to collaborate in a rather more structured manner, particularly where a complex new process needs to be mastered (Skehill 2003). The introduction of new child protection procedures, for example, may be addressed by an agency through formal training sessions which may not afford workers the time to absorb all the implications of proposed changes to the practice environment. By working together in a collaborative learning environment, workers can share their understanding and at times their confusion! This can be a productive process for workers as the load is shared across the group in terms of the information to be learned and disseminated.

Formal Learning through Post-Qualifying Education. With the increasing attention being paid to formal means of registering the activities of social care professionals, there is now considerably more emphasis placed on the continuing education of workers. Within the UK, for example, ongoing registration with the relevant care commission will attempt to ensure that workers maintain an interest in and commitment to ongoing education and training. Most countries now have a range of post-qualifying courses leading to formal qualifications, including those of a vocational nature. Part of the impetus for such developments is a belief that this is the most effective means of encouraging a learning culture within social work organisations.

Bibliography

Abbott, P. and Wallace C. (1997), *An Introduction to Sociology: Feminist Perspectives*, 2nd edn. London: Routledge.

Adams, R. (1996), *Social Work and Empowerment*. London: Palgrave Macmillan.

Adams, R. (1998), *Quality Social Work*. London: Macmillan.

Adams, R., Dominelli, L. and Payne, M. (2002), *Social Work Themes, Issues and Critical Debates*. Basingstoke: Palgrave Macmillan.

Ahmad, B. (1990) *Black Perspectives in Social Work*. Birmingham: Venture Press.

Alaszewski, A. and Manthorpe, J. (1990), 'Literature Review: The New Right and the Professions', *British Journal of Social Work*, Vol. 20, pp. 237–51.

Alcock, P., Erskine, A., May, M. (eds) (2003), *The Student's Companion to Social Policy*. London: Blackwell.

Anderson, J. (1996), 'Yes, But is it Empowerment? Initiation, Implementation and Community Action', in Humphries, B. (ed.), *Critical Perspectives on Empowerment*. Birmingham: Venture Press.

Aquilera, D. (1998), *Crisis Intervention: Theory and Methodology*. New York: Mosby.

Atherton, J. (1986), *Supervision in Residential Care*. London: Tavistock/Routledge.

Bailey, R. and Brake, M. (eds) (1975), *Radical Social Work and Practice*. London: Edward Arnold.

Bandura, A. (1971), *Social Learning Theory*. New York: General Learning Press.

Banks, S. (2001), *Ethics and Values in Social Work*. Basingstoke: Palgrave Macmillan.

Banks, S. (2004), *Ethics, Accountability and the Social Professions*. Basingstoke: Palgrave Macmillan.

Barnes, G. G. (1998), *Family Therapy in Changing Times*. London: Macmillan.

Barry, M. (1998), *Social Exclusion and Social Work: Issues of Theory, Policy and Practice*. Lyme Regis: Russell House Publishing.

Bartlett, W. and Legrand, J. (1993), *Quasi Markets and Social Policy*. Basingstoke: Macmillan.

Beaumont, B. (1999), 'Risk Assessment and Prediction Research', in Parsloe, P. (1999), *Risk Assessment in Social Work and Social Care: Research Highlights 36*. London: Jessica Kingsley.

Becker, H. (1963), *Outsiders: Studies in the Sociology of Deviance*. London: Macmillan.

Bee, H. and Boyd, D. (2003), *Lifespan Development*. Harlow: Pearson Educational.

Beresford, P. (2001), 'Critical Commentaries: Service Users', *British Journal of Social Work*, Vol. 31, pp. 629–30.

Beresford, P. and Wilson, A. (2000), 'Anti-Oppressive Practice: Emancipation or Appropriation?', *British Journal of Social Work*, Vol. 30, pp. 553–73.

Bilson, A. and Ross, S. (1999), *Social Work Management and Practice: Systems Principles*, 2nd edn. London: Jessica Kingsley.

Bloom, M. and Fischer, J. (1982), *Evaluating Practice: Guidelines for the Accountable Professional*. Englewood Cliffs, NJ: Prentice Hall.

Bradley, G. and Manthorpe, J. (2000), *Working on the Faultline*. Birmingham, British Association of Social Workers.

Braye, S. and Preston-Shoot, M. (1995), *Empowering Practice in Social Care*. Buckingham, Open University Press.

Braye, S. and Preston-Shoot, M. (1998), *Practising Social Work Law*. Basingstoke: Macmillan.

Brearley, C. P. (1982), *Risk and Social Work*. London: Routledge & Kegan Paul.

Brearley, J. (1995), Counselling and Social Work. Buckingham: Open University Press.

Brook, E. and Davis, A. (1985) (eds), *Women, the Family and Social Work*. London: Tavistock.

Brown, A. (1992), *Groupwork*, 3rd edn. Aldershot: Ashgate.

Bullock, R., Brown, E., Hobson, C. and Little, M. (1998), *Making Residential Care Work, Structure and Culture in Children's Homes*. Aldershot: Ashgate.

Burman, E. (1994), *Deconstructing Developmental Psychology*. London: Routledge.

Caplan, G. (1964), *Approach to Community Mental Health*. London: Tavistock.

Challis, D., Chesterman, J. and Luckett, R. (2002), *Care Management in Social and Primary Health Care: The Gateshead Community Care Scheme*. Aldershot: Ashgate.

Charles, M. and Butler, S. (2004), 'Social Workers' Management of Organisational Change', in Lymbery, M. and Butler, S., *Social Work Ideals and Practice Realities*. Basingstoke: Palgrave Macmillan.

Cheetham, J. and Kazi, M. (1998), *The Working of Social Work*. London: Jessica Kingsley.

Cigno, K. (2002), 'Cognitive–Behavioural Practice', in Adams, R., Dominelli, L. and Payne, M., *Social Work Themes, Issues and Critical Debates*. Basingstoke: Palgrave Macmillan.

Clarke, J. and Newman, J. (1997), *The Managerial State: Power and Ideology in the Remaking of Social Welfare*. London: Sage.

Clegg, S. R. (1990), *Modern Organisations: Organisation Studies in the Postmodern World*. London: Sage.

Clyde, Lord (1992), *Report of the Inquiry into the Removal of Children from Orkney*. Edinburgh: Scottish Office.

Compton, B. and Galloway, B. (1989), *Social Work Processes*. Homewood: Dorsey Press.

Corden, J. and Preston-Shoot, M. (1987), 'Contract or Con Trick? A Reply to Rojek and Collins', *British Journal of Social Work*, Vol. 17, pp. 535–43.

Corrigan, P. and Leonard, P. (1978), *Social Work Under Capitalism*. London: Macmillan.

Coulshed, V. (1991), *Social Work Practice: An Introduction*, 2nd edn. London: Macmillan.

Coulshed, V. and Orme, J. (1998), *Social Work Practice: An Introduction*, 3rd edn. London: Macmillan.

Dalgleish, L. (2000), 'Assessing the Situation and Deciding to Do Something: Risks, Needs and Consequences', 13th International Congress on Child Abuse and Neglect, Durban (3–6 Sept.) *Proceedings of the 13th IPSCN Conference*. IPSCN: South Africa, pp. 1–18.

Dalley, G. (1996), *Ideologies of Caring: Rethinking Community and Collectivism*, 2nd edn. London: Macmillan.

Dalrymple, J. and Burke, B. (1995), *Anti-oppressive Practice, Social Care and the Law*. London: Open University Press.

Davies, H. and Kinloch, H. (2000), 'Critical Incident Analysis: Facilitating Reflection and Transfer of Learning' in Cree, V. E. and Macauley, C. (eds), *Transfer of Learning in Professional and Vocational Education*. London: Routledge.

Davies, M. (1994), *The Essential Social Worker: An Introduction to Professional Practice in the 1990s*, 3rd edn. London: Arena.

Deacon, A. (2002), *Perspective on Welfare: Ideas, Ideologies, and Policy Debates*. Buckingham: Open University Press.

de Shazer, S. (1982), *Patterns of Brief Family Therapy*. New York: Guilford.

Dewey, J. (1933), *'How We Think'*, *A Restatement of the Relation of Reflective Thinking to the Educative Process*. Chicago: Henrey Regney.

DHSS (Department of Health and Social Security) (1985), *Social Work Decisions in Child Care: Recent Research Findings and their Implications*. London: HMSO.

Dickens, P. (1995), *Quality and Excellence in Human Services*. Chichester, Wiley.

Doel, M. (1992), *Task-Centred Social Work*. Aldershot: Ashgate.

Doel, M. (2002), 'Task Centred Work', in Adams, R., Dominelli, L. and Payne, M., *Social Work Themes, Issues and Critical Debates*. Basingstoke: Palgrave Macmillan.

Doel, M. and Marsh, P. (1992), *Task-Centred Social Work*. England: Ashgate.

Doel, M. and Sawdon, C. (1999), *The Essential Groupworker*. London: Jessica Kingsley.

DOH (Department of Health) (2000), *Framework for the Assessment of Children in Need and their Families*. London: The Stationery Office.

Dominelli, L. (1991), *Anti-Racist Social Work*. Basingstoke: Macmillan.

Dominelli, L. (1998), 'Anti-Oppressive Practice in Social Work', in Adams, R., Dominelli, L. and Payne, M., *Social Work: Themes, Issues and Critical Debates*. Basingstoke: Palgrave Macmillan.

Bibliography

lli, L. (2002a), *Anti-oppressive Social Work Theory and Practice*. Basingstoke: Palgrave millan.

inelli, L. (2002b), *Feminist Social Work Theory and Practice*. Basingstoke: Palgrave Macmillan.

Dominelli, L. and Hoogevelt, A. (1996), 'Globalisation and the Technocratization of Social Work', *Critical Social Policy*, Vol. 16 (2).

Douglas, T. (1993), *A Theory of Groupwork Practice*. London: Macmillan.

Dreyfus, H., Dreyfus, E. and Athanasiou, T. (1986), *Mind over Machine: The Power of Human Intuition and Expertise in the Era of the Computer*. Oxford: Blackwell.

Drummond, H. (1993), *The Quality Movement*. London: Kogan Page.

Dubois, B., Krogsrud, M. K. and O'Malia, M. (1992), *Generalist Social Work Practice: An Empowering Approach*. Englewood Cliffs, NJ: Allyn & Bacon.

Dullea, K. and Mullender, A. (1999), 'Evaluation and Empowerment', in Shaw, I. and Lishman, J. (eds) *Evaluation and Social Work Practice*. London: Sage.

Eby, M. (2000), in A. Brechin, H. Brown and M. Eby, *Critical Practice in Health and Social Care*. Buckingham: Open University.

Erikson, E. (1963), *Childhood and Society*. Harmondsworth: Penguin.

Evans, D. and Kearney, J. (1996), *Working in Social Care: A Systemic Approach*. Aldershot: Ashgate.

Evans, T. and Harris, J. (2004), 'Citizenship, Social Inclusion and Confidentiality', *British Journal of Social Work*, Vol. 34, pp. 69–91.

Everitt, A. and Hardicker, P. (1996), *Evaluating for Good Practice*. London: BASW/Macmillan.

Fernando, S. (1995), *Mental Health in a Multi-Ethnic Society: A Multi-Disciplinary Handbook*. London: Routledge.

Fisher, T. and Somerton, J. (2000), 'Reflection on Action: The Process of Helping Social Work Students Develop their Use of Theory in Practice', *Social Work Education*, Vol. 19, pp. 387–401.

Flynn, N. (1997), *Public Sector Management*, 3rd edn. Hertfordshire: Prentice Hall Harvester.

Fook, J. (ed.) (1996), *The Reflective Researcher: Social Workers' Theories of Practice Research*. St Leonard's, NSW: Allen & Unwin.

Fook, J. (2000), 'Deconstructing and Reconstructing Professional Expertise', in Fawcett, B. Featherstone, B., Fook, J. and Rossiter, A. (eds), *Postmodern Feminist Perspectives*. London: Routledge.

Fook, J. (2002), *Social Work: Critical Theory and Practice*. London: Sage.

Ford, K. and Jones, A. (1987), *Student Supervision*. Basingstoke: Macmillan.

Ford, P. and Postle, K. (2000), 'Task-Centred Practice and Care Management', in Stepney, P. and Ford, D., *Social Work Models, Methods and Theories: A Framework for Practice*. Lyme Regis: Russell House Publishing.

Frost, N. (2002), 'Evaluating Practice', in Adams, R., Dominelli, L. and Payne, M. (eds), *Critical Practice in Social Work*. Basingstoke: Palgrave Macmillan.

Ghayle, T. and Lillyman, S. (1997), *Learning Journals and Critical Incidents: Reflective Practice for Health Care Professionals*. Wilts: Quay Books.

Gibbs, G. (1988), *Learning by Doing: A Guide to Teaching and Learning Methods*. Further Education Unit: Oxford Polytechnic.

Glendinning, C. and Millar, J. (1992), *Women and Poverty in Britain: The 1990s*. Brighton: Harvester Wheatsheaf.

Goldberg, E. M., Gibbons, J. and Sinclair, I. (1977), *Problems, Tasks and Outcomes: The Evaluation of Task-Centred Casework in Three Settings*. National Institute Social Services Library, No. 47: Allen & Unwin.

Goldberg, E. M., Gibbons, J. and Sinclair, I. (1985), *Problems, Tasks and Outcomes*, 2nd edn. London: George Allen & Unwin.

Goldstein, H. (1981), *Social Learning and Change: A Cognitive Approach to Social Work Practice*. New York: Tavistock.

GSCC (General Social Care Council) (2002), *Codes of Practice for Social Care Workers and Employers*. London: GSCC.

Hackett, S. and Marsland, P. (1997), 'Perceptions of Power: An Exploration of Power Dynamics in the Student–Tutor–Practice–Teacher Relationship within Child Protection Placements', *Social Work Education*, Vol. 16 (2), pp. 44–61.

Hamner, J. and Stratham, D. (1999), *Women and Social Work: Towards a Woman-Centred Practice*. London: Macmillan.

Handy, C. (1993), *Understanding Organisations*, 4th edn. Harmondsworth: Penguin.

Haralambos, M., Heald, R. M., Holborn, M. (2004), *Sociology Themes and Perspectives*, 5th edn. London: Collins Educational.

Hawkins, P. and Shohet, R. (2000), *Supervision in the Helping Professions*. Buckingham: Open University Press.

Healy, K. (2000), *Social Work Practices: Contemporary Perspectives on Change*. London: Sage.

Hill, M. and Laing, P. (1979), *Social Work and Money*. London: Allen & Unwin.

HMSO (2000), *Care Standards Act 2000*. London: Stationery Office.

Hollis, F. (1964), (1st edn.) *Casework: A Psychosocial Therapy*. New York: Random House.

Hollis, F. (1972), *Casework: A Psychosocial Therapy*, 2nd edn. New York: Random House.

Howe, D. (1987), *An Introduction to Social Work Theory: Making Sense in Practice*. London: Arena.

Howe, D. (1995), *Attachment Theory for Social Work Practice*. Basingstoke: Macmillan.

Howe, D. (1996), 'Surface and Depth in Social Work Practice', in Parton, N. (ed.), *Social Theory, Social Change and Social Work*. London: Routledge.

Howe, D. (2002), 'Psychosocial Work', in Adams, R., Dominelli, L. and Payne, M., *Social Work Themes, Issues and Critical Debates*. Basingstoke: Palgrave Macmillan.

Hudson, B. (1994), 'Behavioural Social Work', in Lishman, J., *Handbook of Theory for Social Work*. London: Jessica Kingsley.

Hudson, B. and MacDonald, G. (1986), *Behavioural Social Work: An Introduction*. London: Macmillan.

Hugman, R. (1991), *Power in Caring Professions*. London: Palgrave Macmillan.

Ixer, G. (1999), 'There's No Such Thing as Reflection', *British Journal of Social Work*, Vol. 29, pp. 513–27.

Jacobs, M. (1994), 'Psychodynamic Counselling', in Lishman, J., *Handbook of Theory for Practice Teachers in Social Work*. London: Jessica Kingsley.

James, A. (1994), *Managing to Care: Public Services and the Market*. London: Longman.

Jones, C. (2001), 'Voices from the Front Line: State Social Workers and New Labour', *British Journal of Social Work*, Vol. 31, pp. 547–62.

Jordan, B. (2004), Emancipatory Social Work? Opportunity or Oxymoron, *British Journal of Social Work*, Vol. 34, pp. 5–19.

Kadushin, A. and Harkness, D. (2002), *Supervision in Social Work*. New York: Columbia University Press.

Kazi, M. A. F. (1998), *Single-Case Evaluation by Social Workers*. Aldershot: Ashgate.

Kelly, G. (1996), 'Competence in Risk Analysis', in O'Hagan, K., *Competence in Social Work Practice: A Guide for Professionals*. London: Jessica Kingsley.

Langan, M. and Day, L. (eds) (1992), *Women, Oppression and Social Work*. London: Routledge.

Langan, M. and Lee, P. (1989), *Radical Social Work Today*. London: Routledge.

Lewin, K. (1987), 'Team Development', in Payne, M. *Working in Teams*. London: Macmillan.

Lindemann, E. (1944), 'Symptomatology and Management of Acute Grief', *American Journal of Psychiatry*, Vol. 101, pp. 141–8.

Lishman, J. (1994), *Communication in Social Work*. Basingstoke: Macmillan.

Lloyd, M. and Taylor, C. (1995), 'From Florence Hollis to the Orange Book: Developing a Holistic Model of Social Work Assessment in the 1990s', *British Journal of Social Work*, Vol. 25, pp. 691–710.

Lymbery, M. (2001), Social Work at the Crossroads, *British Journal of Social Work*, Vol. 31, pp. 369–84.

Lymbery, M. (2004), 'Responding to Crisis: The Changing Nature of Social Work Organisations', in Lymbery, M. and Butler, S., *Social Work: Ideals and Practice Realities*. Basingstoke: Palgrave Macmillan.

Lymbery, M. and Butler, S. (2004), *Social Work Ideals and Practice Realities*. Basingstoke: Palgrave Macmillan.

Lyons, K. and Manion, H. (2004), 'Goodbye DipSW: Trends in Student Satisfaction and Employment Outcomes. Some Implications for the New Social Work Award', *Social Work Education*, Vol. 23, pp. 133–48.

Marsh, P. (1994), 'Task Centred Practice', in Lishman, J. (ed.), *Handbook of Theory for Practice Teachers in Social Work*. London: Jessica Kingsley.

Marsh, P. (1997), 'Task Centred Work', in *The Blackwell Companion to Social Work*. Oxford: Blackwell.

Marsh, P. and Triseliotis, J. (1996), *Ready to Practise? Social Workers and Probation Officers: Their Training and First Year in Work*. Avebury: Aldershot.

Mayer, J. E. and Timms, N. (1970), *'The Client Speaks': Working Class Impressions of Casework*. London: Routledge.

McGuire, J. (1995), *What Works: Reducing Re-offending, Guidelines from Research and Practice*. Chichester: Wiley.

McGuire, J. (2000), *Cognitive Behavioural Approaches: An Introduction to Theory and Research*. London: Home Office.

McGuire, J. and Priestley, P. (1995), 'Reviewing "What Works": Past, Present and Future', in McGuire, J. (ed.), *What Works: Reducing Reoffending–Guidelines from Research and Practice* (pp. 3–34).Toronto: Wiley.

McIvor, G., Moodie, K., Perrott, S. and Spencer, F. (2001), 'The Relative Effectiveness of Risk Assessment Instruments', *Social Work Research Findings No. 40*. Edinburgh: Scottish Executive Central Research Unit.

Milner, J. (2001), *Women and Social Work, Narrative Approaches*. Basingstoke: Palgrave Macmillan.

Milner, J. and O'Byrne, P. (1998), *Assessment in Social Work*. Basingstoke: Palgrave Macmillan.

Milner, J. and O'Byrne, P. (2002) (2nd edn), *Assessment in Social Work*. Basingstoke: Palgrave Macmillan.

Mitchell, S. (2000), *Modernising Social Services: The Management Challenge in the 1998 Social Service White Paper in Local Authority Social Services*. London: Blackwell.

Mullaly, R. (1997), *Structural Social Work: Ideology, Theory and Practice*. New York: Oxford University Press.

Munro, L. (2001), 'Empowering Looked After Children', *Child and Family Social Work*, Vol. 6, pp. 129–37.

NISW (National Institute for Social Work) (1996), *'The Standards We Expect'*. London: HMSO.

Office of the Deputy Prime Minister (2004), *Strategic Partnering Taskforce Final Report*. Wetherby: ODPM Publications.

O'Hagan, K. (1986), 'There isn't an Effective Crisis Training Program', *Social Work Today*, 29 September.

O'Hagan, K. (1986), *Crisis Intervention in Social Services*. London: Macmillan.

Orme, J. (1995), *Workloads: Measurement and Management*. Aldershot: Avebury.

Orme, J. (2001), *Gender and Community Care: Social Work and Social Care Perspectives*. Basingstoke: Macmillan.

Orme, J. and Glastonbury, B. (1994), *Care Management: Tasks and Workloads*. Basingstoke: Macmillan.

O'Sullivan, T. (1999), *Decision Making in Social Work*. Basingstoke: Palgrave Macmillan.

Parker, J. and Bradley, G. (2003), *Social Work Practice: Assessment, Planning, Intervention and Review*. Exeter: Learning Matters.

Parrott, L. (1999), *Social Work and Social Care*. Gildredge Press: East Sussex.

Parton, N. (1985), *The Politics of Child Abuse*. London: Macmillan.

Parton, N. (1996), *Social Theory, Social Change and Social Work*. London: Routledge.

Parton, N. and O'Byrne, P. (2000), *Constructive Social Work: Towards a New Practice*. London: Palgrave Macmillan.

Payne, M. (1997), *Modern Social Work Theory: A Critical Introduction*. London: Palgrave Macmillan.

Pease, B. and Fook, J. (1999), *Transforming Social Work Practice: Postmodern Critical Perspectives*. London: Routledge.

Pierson, J. and Thomas, M. (2002), *Dictionary of Social Work*. Glasgow: HarperCollins.

Pincus, A. and Minahan, A. (1773), *Social Work Practice: Model and Method*. Itasca, IL: F.E. Peacock.

Popple, K. (1995), *Analysing Community Work: Its Theory and Practice*. Milton Keynes: Open University.

Postle, K. (2002), Working 'Between the Idea and the Reality: Ambiguities and Tensions in Care Managers' Work, *British Journal of Social Work*, Vol. 32, pp. 335–51.

Pratt, T. (2000), 'Decision-making by Senior Social Workers at Point of First Referral', *British Journal of Social Work*, Vol. 30, pp. 597–618.

Preston-Shoot, M. (2001), 'A Triumph of Hope over Experience? On Modernising Accountability in Social Services – The Case for Complaints Procedures in Community Care', *Social Policy and Administration*, Vol. 35, pp. 701–15.

Preston-Shoot, M. and Agass, D. (1990), *Making Sense of Social Work*. Basingstoke: Macmillan.

Prochaska, J. O., DiClemente, C. C. and Norcross, J. C. (1992), 'In Search of How People Change: Applications to Addictive Behaviours', *American Psychologist*, Vol. 47, No. 9, pp. 1102–112.

Pugh, R. and Thompson, N. (1999), 'Social Work Citizenship and Constitutional Change in the UK', in *International Perspectives in Social Work – Social Work and the State*. Brighton: Pavilion.

Quinn, F. M. (2000), 'Reflection and Reflective Practice', in C. Davies, L. Findlay and A. Bullman, *Changing Practice in Health and Social Care*. London: Sage.

Rapoport, L. (1970), 'Crisis Intervention as a Brief Mode of Treatment', in Roberts, R. W. and Nee, R. H. (eds), *Theories of Social Casework*. Chicago: Chicago University Press.

Raynor, P. (1996), 'Effectiveness Now, a Personal and Selective Overview', in McIvor, G. (ed.), *Working with Offenders*. London: Jessica Kingsley.

Reid, W. J. (1978), *The Task-Centred System*. New York: Columbia University Press.

Reid, W. J. and Epstein, L. (1972), *Task-Centred Case Work*. Columbia: Columbia University Press.

Reid, W. J. and Epstein, L. (1977), *Task-Centred Case Work*, 2nd edn. Columbia: Columbia University Press.

Richmond, M. (1922), *Social Diagnosis*, Russell Sage Foundation.

Roberts, A. R. (2000), *Crisis Intervention Handbook: Assessment, Treatment, and Research*. New York: Oxford University Press.

Robinson, L. (1995), *Psychology for Social Workers: Black Perspectives*. London: Routledge.

Rojek, C. and Collins, S. (1988), 'Contract or Con Trick?, *British Journal of Social Work*, Vol. 17, pp. 199–211.

Rowe, J. and Lambert, L. (1973), *Children who Wait*. London: ABAA.

Ruch, G. (2000), 'Self and Social Work: Towards an Integrated Model of Learning', *Journal of Social Work Practice*, Vol. 14, No. 2, pp. 99–112.

Runciman, P. (1989), 'Health Assessment of the Elderly: A Multidisciplinary Perspective', in Taylor, R. and Ford, J. (eds), *Social Work and Health Care*. London: Jessica Kingsley.

Ryan, T. (1993), *Life Story Work*. London: British Agencies for Adoption and Fostering.

Schön, D. A. (1983), *The Reflective Practitioner*. New York: Basic Books.

Schön, D. (1987), *Educating the Reflective Practitioner*. San Francisco: Jossey Bass.

Schön, D. (1991), *The Reflective Practitioner: How Professionals Think in Action*. New York: Basic Books.

Scottish Executive (2001), *Joint Resourcing and Joint Management of Community Care Services*, Circular No: CCD7/2001.

Scottish Office (1997), *Social Work and Criminal Justice: Sentencer Decision-Making*. Edinburgh: The Stationery Office.

Seden, J. (1999), *Counselling Skills in Social Work Practice*. Buckingham: Open University Press.

Seligman, M. (1992), *Helplessness*. New York: Freeman.

Sermeus, W. (2003), 'Information Technology and the Organisation of Patient Care', in Harlow, E. and Webb, S. E. (eds), *Information and Communication Technologies in the Welfare Services*. London: Jessica Kingsley.

Shardlow, S. (2002), 'Ethics, Values and Social Work', in Adams, R., Dominelli, L. and Payne, M., *Social Work Themes, Issues and Critical Debates*. 2nd edn. Basingstoke: Palgrave Macmillan.

Shaw, I. and Lishman, J. (1999), *Evaluation and Social Work Practice*. London: Sage.

Sheldon, B. (1995), *Cognitive Behavioural Therapy; Research Practice and Philosophy*. London: Routledge.

Sheldon, B. and Chilvers, R. (2000), *Evidence-Based Social Care: A Study of Prospects and Problems*. Lyme Regis: Russell House Publishing.

Skehill, C. (2003), 'Using a Peer Action Learning Approach in the Implementation of Communication and Information Technology in Social Work Education', *Social Work Education*, Vol. 22 (2), pp. 177–90.

Smale, G., Tuson, G., Biehal, N. and Marsh, P. (1993), *Empowerment, Assessment, Care Management and the Skilled Worker*. London: NISW and The Stationery Office.

Spencer, P. C., Munch, S. (2003), 'Client Violence toward Social Workers: The Role of Management in Community Mental Health Programs', *Social Work*, Vol. 48, pp. 532–44. NASW.

Spicker, P. (1995), *Social Policy: Themes and Approaches*. London: Prentice Hall.

Stepney, P. and Ford, D. (2000), *Social Work Models, Methods and Theories: A Framework for Practice*. Lyme Regis: Russell House Publishing.

Taylor, B. and Devine, T. (1993), *Assessing Need and Planning Care in Social Work*. Aldershot: Arena.

Thomas, N. and O'Kane, C. (1999), 'Experiences of Decision-making in Middle Childhood: The Example of Children "Looked after" by Local Authorities', *Childhood*, Vol. 6, pp. 369–87.

Thompson, N. (1991), *Crisis Intervention Revisited*. Birmingham: PEPAR Publications.

Thompson, N. (1997), *Anti-Discriminatory Practice*, 2nd edn. Basingstoke: Macmillan.

Thompson, N. (1998), *Promoting Equality: Challenging Discrimination and Oppression in the Human Services*. Basingstoke: Macmillan.

Thompson, N. (2000), *Understanding Social Work: Preparing for Practice*. Basingstoke: Palgrave Macmillan.

Thompson, N. (2002), *People Skills*, 2nd edn. Basingstoke: Palgrave Macmillan.

Tossell, D. and Webb, R. (1986), *Inside the Caring Services*. London: Edward Arnold.

Trevithick, P. (2000), *Social Work Skills: A Practice Handbook*. Buckingham: Open University Press.

Trotter, C. (1999), *Working with Involuntary Clients: A Guide to Practice*. London: Sage.

Twelvetrees, A. (2002), 3rd edn. *Community Work*. London: Macmillan.

Vickery, A. (1977), *Caseload Management: A Guide for Supervisors of Social Work Staff*. London: NISW.

Walker, S. (2004), *Applying Family Therapy: A Guide for Caring Professionals in the Community*. London: Russell House Publishing.

Waterhouse, L., McGhee, J. and Loucks, N. (2004), Disentangling Offenders and Non-Offenders in the Scottish Children's Hearings: A Clear Divide?, *The Howard Journal*, Vol. 43, pp. 164–79.

Watson, D. (2002), 'A Critical Perspective on Quality within the Personal Social Services: Prospects and Concerns', *British Journal of Social Work*, Vol. 38 (2).

Watson, D. (2003), 'The Development of Total Quality Management in the Public and Personal Social Services: Realities, Limitations and Opportunities within the Modernising Agenda?', *Local Government Studies*, Vol. 29 (2).

Watson, D. and West, J. (2003), 'The Role of the Tutor in Social Work Education: Building an Emancipatory Tutorial Relationship', *Social Work Education*, Vol. 22 (2), pp. 139–50.

West, J. and Watson, D. (2002), 'Preparing for Practice: The Use of Personal Learning Audits in Social Work Education', *Practice*, Vol. 14(4).

White, V. (1999), 'Feminist Social Work and the State: A British Perspective', in *International Perspectives in Social Work – Social Work and the State*. Brighton: Pavilion.

Index

Abbott, P., 8
ABC assessment of behaviour, 83–4
access to information, 47
accountability, 67, 137–8, 139
action learning sets, 171
active listening, 45, 46
Adams, R., 3, 5, 152, 166, 167
Agass, D., 141
agency issues
  and approaches to practice, 13–14, 28
  and method selection, 115–17
Ahmad, B., 61, 79
Alaszewski, A., 115
Alcock, P., 25
Anderson, J., 3
anti-oppressive practice, 3, 5, 20, 43–4, 143
approaches to practice, 12–29
  individual pathology approach, 17–19
  influence on method selection, 59–62,
    117–20
  knowledge for practice, 14–15, 27–8,
    160–1
  and modern social work, 165–71
  practice theories, 24–7
  procedural approach, 15–17
  progressive approach, 19–21
  reflecting on personal approach, 21–3
  skills needed, 161–3
  and understanding of personal and
    professional values, 14
  and understanding of society, 12–13
  and understanding of wider political and
    agency issues, 13–14
Aquilera, D., 101, 108
assessment, 30–50
  action stage, 33
  in behavioural social work, 83–5
  biography framework, 56–7
  and communication skills, 44–7
  in crisis intervention, 104–5
  exchange model, 41–2, 43, 57
  and honesty and openness, 43
  influence of models on approach, 40–4
  meeting service user, 31–2
  and methods of intervention, 56–8,
    114–15

and negotiation skills, 47–8
as ongoing activity, 34
and partnership, 38–40, 47, 48
preparation for meeting service user, 30–1
procedural model, 40–1, 42, 43
in psychosocial casework, 94–5
questioning model, 40, 41, 42, 43
reflection and analysis stage, 32–3
of risk, 35–40
and screening referrals for resources, 33
in task-centred casework, 75–7
Atherton, J., 138
autonomy of social worker, undermining
  of, 5–6

Bailey, R., 52
Bandura, A., 101
Banks, S., 14, 32, 138, 142, 143
Barry, M., 3
Bartlett, W., 166
Beaumont, B., 38
Becker, H., 16
behavioural social work, 82–9
  assessment, 83–5
  concerns with, 88–9
  issues for, 87–8
  process of implementation, 58, 85–6
  selection of, 59–60, 111, 112
  termination and evaluation, 86–7
  theory, 82–3
Beresford, P., 3, 12
Bloom, M., 153
Bradley, G., 32–3, 111, 142, 170
Brake, M., 52
Braye, S., 13, 24, 39, 115, 161, 168
Brearley, C. P., 37–8
'Brian', 34–5, 93–4, 102, 150–1
Brook, E., 18
Bullock, R., 28, 58
Burke, B., 4, 21, 24, 35, 38, 43, 56, 168
Burman, E., 25
Butler, S., 9, 12, 19, 51, 64

Caplan, G., 100, 101, 103, 104
care management, 51, 52–3, 55–6
caseload management, 63–6